Name ______________________________

Reading and Writing Numbers

Practice 1.1

Circle groups of ten.
Write the number.
Draw a line to the correct number word.

1. 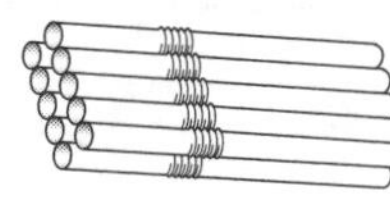  30 — twenty-six

2. 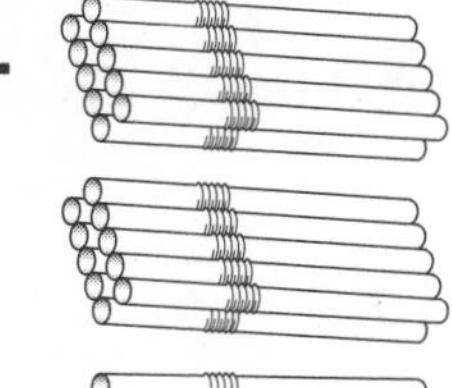 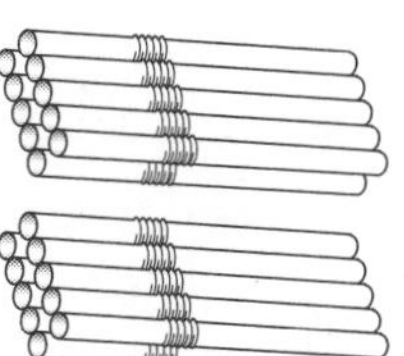 ____ — fifty

3. 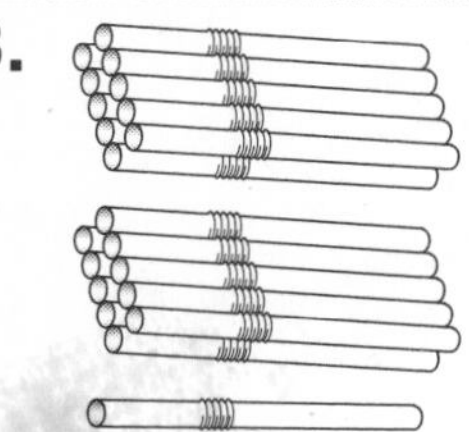 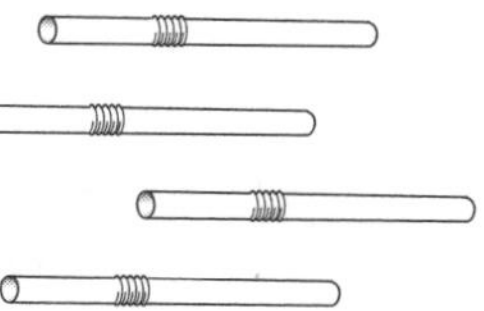 ____ — th…

forty-two

4. 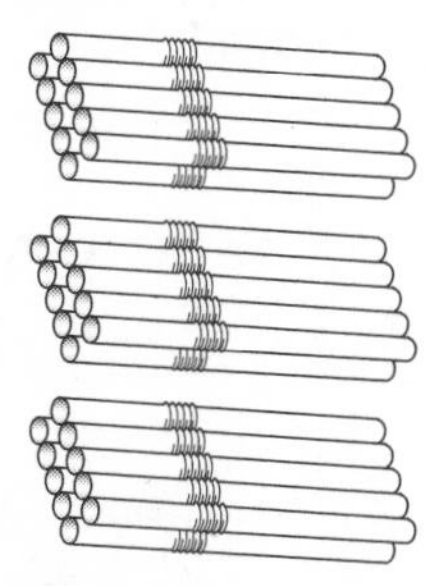 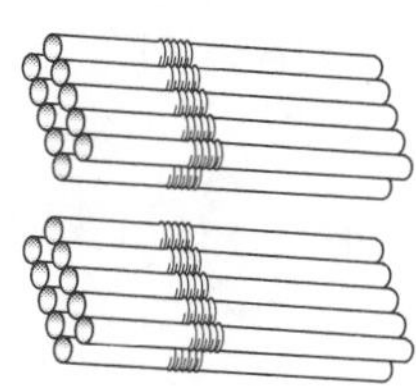 ____

Test Prep

Fill in the ○ for the correct answer. NH means Not Here.

5. How many straws are there?

45	43	34	NH
○	○	○	○

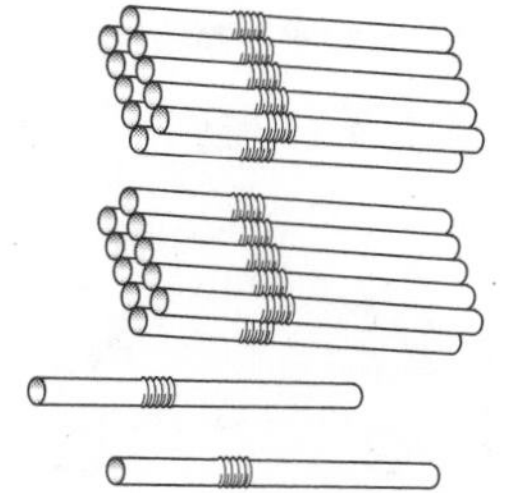 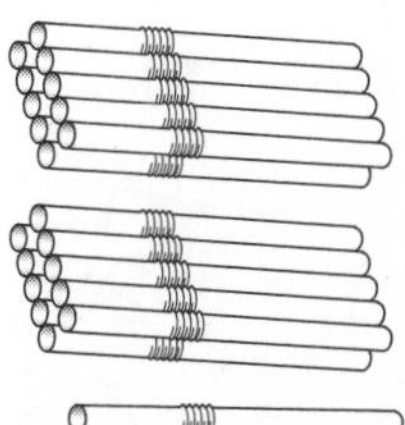

Name ________________ Date ________

Practice 1.2

Ordering Numbers

Use the number line below.
Complete the sentence.

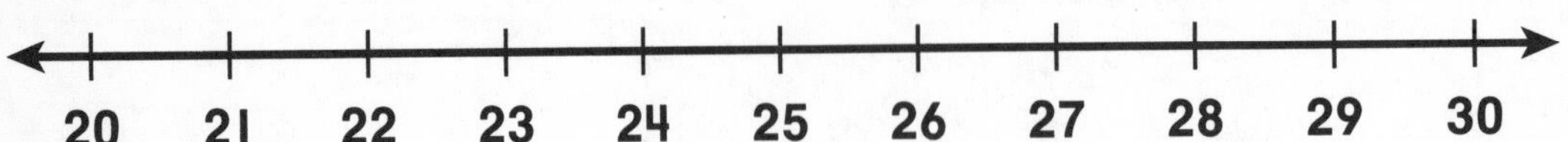

1. 24 is just before 25
2. 26 is just after ____
3. 29 is one less than ____
4. ____ is one more than 27
5. 23 is just after ____
6. ____ is just before 22

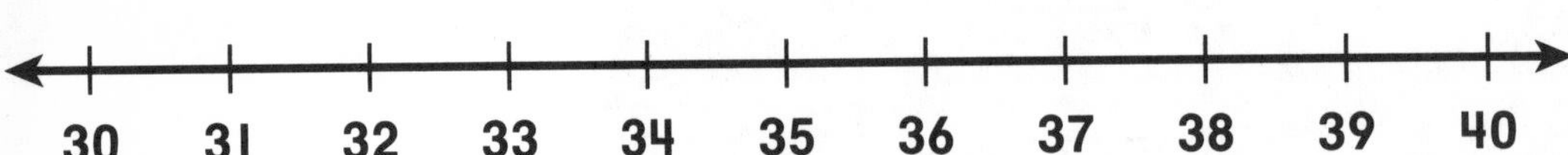

Count forward.
Write the missing numbers.

7. 33, 34, ____, ____, 37

Count backward.
Write the missing numbers.

8. 36, 35, ____, 33, ____

Test Prep

Fill in the ○ for the correct answer. NH means Not Here.

9. Which number comes just after 21?

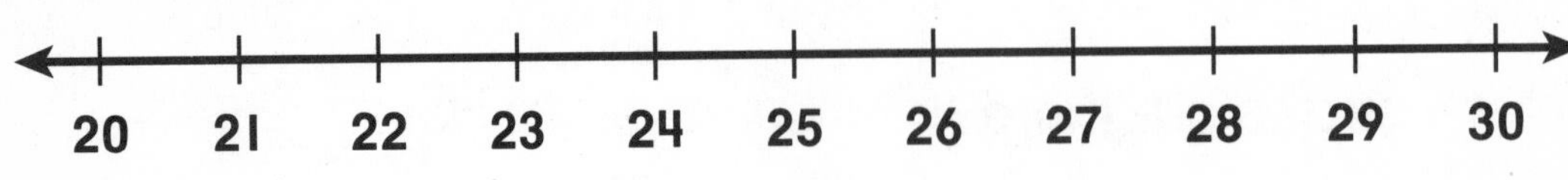

25	23	22	NH
○	○	○	○

Use with text pages 11–12.

Name ______________________ Date ______________

Practice 1.3

Comparing Numbers

Write how many.
Circle the greater number.
Write more or fewer.

1.  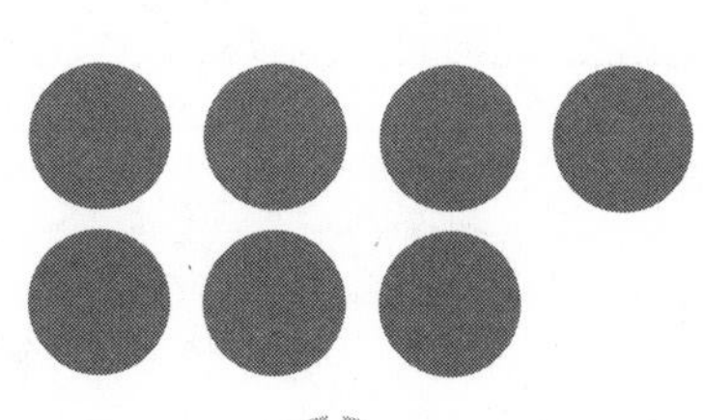

There are  ______ than .

5 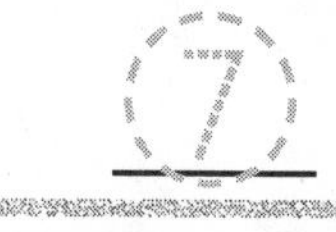

2. 

There are ______

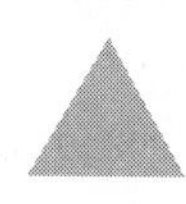 than 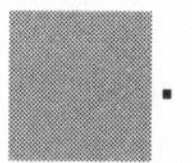.

______ ______

Write > or <.

3. 36 ◯ 25 **4.** 45 ◯ 49 **5.** 12 ◯ 11

6. 24 ◯ 29 **7.** 19 ◯ 15 **8.** 42 ◯ 44

9. I am less than 18.
I am greater than 16.
What number am I? ______

Test Prep

Fill in the ○ for the correct answer. NH means Not Here.

10. Which number sentence is true?

42 > 52	31 > 25	19 > 31	NH
○	○	○	○

Name ______________________ Date ______________

Practice 1.4

Estimating How Many

Estimate how many.

You can circle a group of ten to help you. Think about how many tens in all.

1. 

Estimate: about 30–35

2. 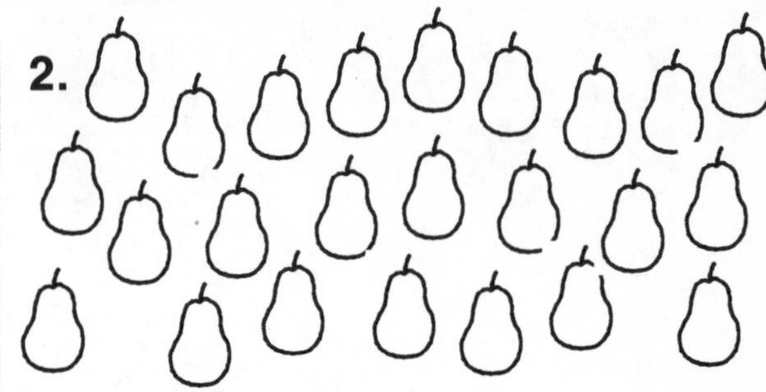

Estimate: about ____________

3. 

Estimate: about ____________

4. 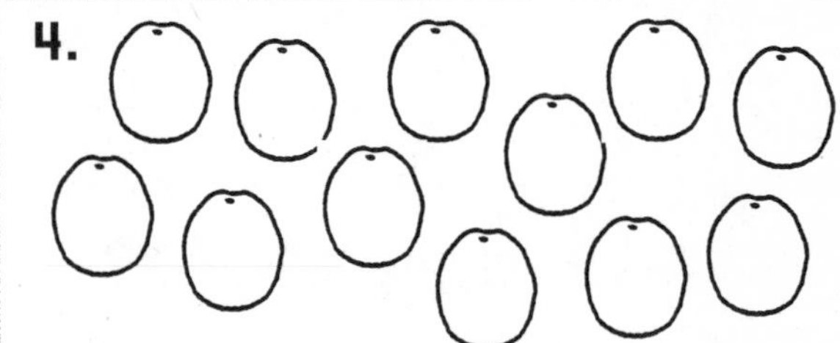

Estimate: about ____________

5. About how many are there? Circle the best estimate.

about 30 about 50 about 70

Test Prep

Fill in the ○ for the correct answer. NH means Not Here.

6. Estimate how many.

10–15	20–25	30–35	NH
○	○	○	○

Explain how you chose your estimate.

Name ______________________ Date __________

Practice 1.5

Decision: Reasonable Answers

Circle the most reasonable answer.

Draw or write to explain.

1. There are 8 children playing soccer. Then 2 leave to go home. Are there more children or fewer children playing soccer?

   no children more children

   fewer children

2. Olivia plays hoop ball. She has 5 balls to throw in a hoop. She gets the first 3 in the hoop. How many throws does she have left?

   none 2 throws 3 throws

3. There are 5 children in the park. Then 4 other children come to play. Are there more children or fewer children playing?

   10 children more children

   fewer children

Test Prep

Fill in the ○ for the correct answer. NH means Not Here.

4. Ruby strings 4 beads. Jake strings 3 beads. Does Ruby string more beads or fewer beads than Jake?

   ○ 7 beads ○ more beads ○ fewer beads ○ NH

Name ______________________ Date ______________

Addition Properties

Add.

1. 5 + 3 = 8 3 + 5 = 8

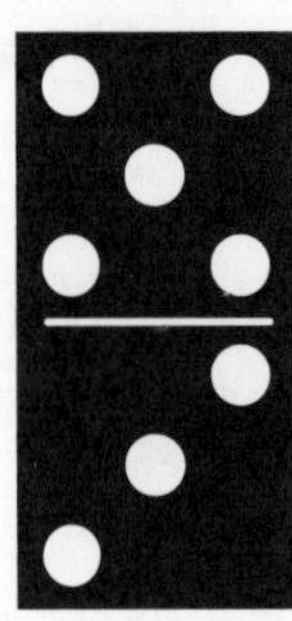

2. 0 + 4 = ____ 4 + 0 = ____

3. 7 + 2 = ____ 2 + 7 = ____

4. 3 + 1 = ____ 1 + 3 = ____

5. 4 + 0 = ____ 0 + 4 = ____

6. 0 + 5 = ____

7. 1 + 5 = ____

8. 6 + 3 = ____

9. 4 + 2 = ____

10. 1 + 7 = ____

11. 7 + 0 = ____

12. 8 + 1 = ____

13. 8 + 2 = ____

14. 0 + 6 = ____

Test Prep

Fill in the ○ for the correct answer. NH means Not Here.

15. 6 + 4 = ____ + 6

4 ○ 6 ○ 10 ○ NH ○

Use with text pages 27–28.

Name ____________________ Date ____________

Count On to Add

Use the number line.
Count on to add.

Remember
Start with the greater number.

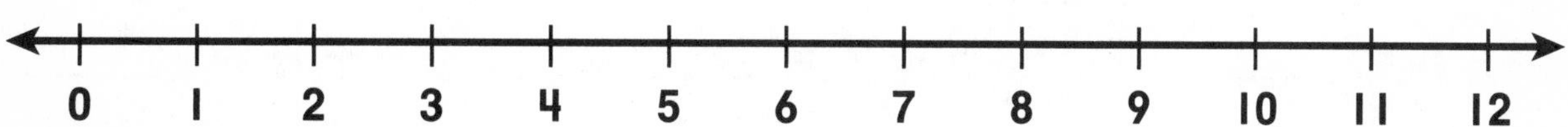

1. $7 + 2 =$ 9
2. $4 + 3 =$ ____
3. $9 + 2 =$ ____
4. ____ $= 8 + 2$
5. ____ $= 4 + 2$
6. ____ $= 11 + 1$
7. $4 + 5$
8. $5 + 6$
9. $10 + 2$
10. $7 + 1$
11. $2 + 5$
12. $3 + 8$
13. $2 + 9$
14. $9 + 1$

Test Prep

Fill in the ○ for the correct answer. NH means Not Here.

15. Solve.

$4 + 8 =$ ____

12	11	4	NH
○	○	○	○

Name ______________________ Date ____________

Practice 2.3

Use Doubles Facts

Find the sum.
Use doubles facts and doubles-plus-one facts.

1. 6 + 6 = 12　　6 + 7 = ____　　7 + 6 = ____

2. 8 + 8 = ____　　8 + 9 = ____　　9 + 8 = ____

3. $\begin{array}{r} 5 \\ +5 \\ \hline \end{array}$　　$\begin{array}{r} 5 \\ +6 \\ \hline \end{array}$　　$\begin{array}{r} 9 \\ +9 \\ \hline \end{array}$　　$\begin{array}{r} 10 \\ +9 \\ \hline \end{array}$

4. $\begin{array}{r} 7 \\ +7 \\ \hline \end{array}$　　$\begin{array}{r} 7 \\ +8 \\ \hline \end{array}$　　$\begin{array}{r} 3 \\ +3 \\ \hline \end{array}$　　$\begin{array}{r} 3 \\ +4 \\ \hline \end{array}$

Write a double.
Use the double to complete the doubles-plus-one fact.

Double	Double-plus-one
5. ____ + ____ = 8	____ + ____ = 9

Test Prep

Fill in the ○ for the correct answer. NH means Not Here.

6. Which double can help you find 8 + 7?

4 + 4 ○　　5 + 5 ○　　6+ 6 ○　　NH ○

Name ______________________ Date __________

Add 10

Use Workmat 1 with ⬬.

Add.

Think about how adding 10 changes a number.

1. 10 + 5 = 15 2. 10 + 2 = ____ 3. 7 + 10 = ____

4. 9 + 10 = ____ 5. 7 + 3 = ____ 6. 10 + 3 = ____

7. 10 + 0 8. 10 + 8 9. 7 + 10 10. 4 + 10

11. 10 + 6 12. 8 + 10 13. 1 + 10 14. 2 + 10

15. 3 + 10 16. 10 + 10 17. 5 + 10 18. 10 + 9

Test Prep

Fill in the ○ for the correct answer. NH means Not Here.

19. Solve.

____ + 10 = 14

10	4	0	NH
○	○	○	○

Name ____________ Date ____________

Practice 2.5

Make 10 to Add

Add.

Remember
Make 10 before you add.

1. $8 + 5 =$ 13
2. $9 + 7 =$
3. $6 + 7 =$
4. $9 + 8 =$
5. $4 + 9 =$
6. $5 + 7 =$
7. $8 + 6 =$
8. $6 + 9 =$

Complete each addition sentence.

9.

10 + ____ = 17

____ + 8 = 17

7 + ____ = 17

8 + 9 = ____

10.

____ + 3 = 13

6 + ____ = 13

8 + 5 = ____

9 + ____ = 13

11.

____ + 2 = 12

8 + ____ = 12

3 + ____ = 12

7 + 5 = ____

Test Prep

Fill in the ○ for the correct answer. NH means Not Here.

12. Which number completes the number sentence?

____ + 9 = 15

8	7	6	NH
○	○	○	○

Use with text pages 37–38.

Name ______________________ Date ____________

Practice 2.6

Add Three Numbers

Find the sum.
Look for two numbers to add first.

Look for ways to make a 10 first.

1. $6 + 9 + 1 =$ 16

2. $5 + 3 + 7 =$

3. $2 + 7 + 3 =$

4. $5 + 0 + 9 =$

5. $8 + 5 + 2 =$

6. $9 + 4 + 3 =$

7. $4 + 4 + 8 =$

8. $3 + 8 + 7 =$

9. 8 + 8 + 1 = ______

10. 1 + 5 + 6 = ______

11. 7 + 3 + 8 = ______

12. 6 + 3 + 6 = ______

13. 9 + 0 + 9 = ______

14. 4 + 5 + 5 = ______

Test Prep

15. Fill in the ○ for the correct answer. NH means Not Here.
Find the sum.

$7 + 2 + 5$

15	14	9	NH
○	○	○	○

Explain which two numbers you added first and why.

Name ______________________ Date __________

Practice 2.7

Problem Solving
Draw a Picture

You can draw a picture to help you solve a problem.

Draw and write.

1. Rosa has 4 markers, 7 crayons, and 5 pieces of chalk. How many things does she have in all?

   16 things in all

2. The class makes pictures. There are 6 pictures of dinosaurs. There are 3 more pictures of elephants than dinosaurs. How many pictures are there in all?

   ______ pictures

3. Ann makes 4 stars for the mural. Sam makes 1 fewer star than Ann. Willy makes 3 more stars than Ann. How many stars do the friends make in all?

   ______ stars

Use with text pages 41–43.

Name ______________________ Date ____________

Practice 3.1

Subtraction Properties

$5 - 0 = 5$

$5 - 5 = 0$

Subtract.

1. $\begin{array}{r} 15 \\ -15 \\ \hline 0 \end{array}$
2. $\begin{array}{r} 12 \\ -\ 0 \\ \hline \end{array}$
3. $\begin{array}{r} 10 \\ -\ 0 \\ \hline \end{array}$
4. $\begin{array}{r} 8 \\ -8 \\ \hline \end{array}$
5. $\begin{array}{r} 4 \\ -4 \\ \hline \end{array}$
6. $\begin{array}{r} 18 \\ -18 \\ \hline \end{array}$
7. $\begin{array}{r} 11 \\ -\ 0 \\ \hline \end{array}$
8. $\begin{array}{r} 19 \\ -\ 0 \\ \hline \end{array}$
9. $\begin{array}{r} 11 \\ -11 \\ \hline \end{array}$
10. $\begin{array}{r} 19 \\ -19 \\ \hline \end{array}$
11. $\begin{array}{r} 20 \\ -\ 0 \\ \hline \end{array}$
12. $\begin{array}{r} 1 \\ -0 \\ \hline \end{array}$

Test Prep

Fill in the ○ for the correct answer. NH means Not Here.

13. Subtract.

$\begin{array}{r} 20 \\ -\ 0 \\ \hline \end{array}$

______

20	2	0	NH
○	○	○	○

Use with text pages 51–52.

Name ______________________ Date ____________

Practice 3.2

Count Back to Subtract

Use the number line.
Count back to subtract.

Remember
You can use a number line to help you count back.

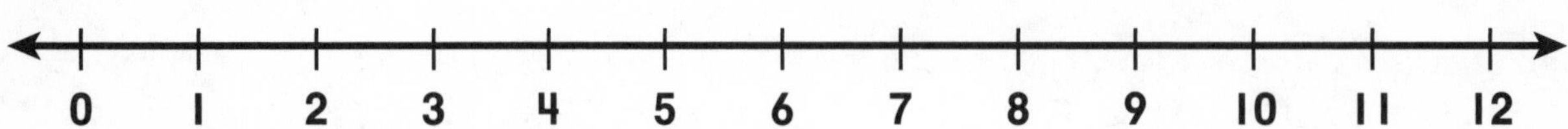

1. 9 − 2 = 7
2. 11 − 1 = ____
3. 10 − 3 = ____
4. 8 − 3 = ____
5. 12 − 1 = ____
6. 6 − 2 = ____
7. 10 − 1 = ____
8. 11 − 3 = ____
9. 5 − 3 = ____
10. 10 − 2
11. 7 − 3
12. 4 − 1
13. 6 − 3
14. 8 − 1
15. 5 − 3
16. 9 − 1
17. 5 − 1

Test Prep

Fill in the ○ for the correct answer. NH means Not Here.

18. Subtract.

12 − 3 = ____

11	10	9	NH
○	○	○	○

Use with text pages 53–54.

Name ______________________ Date ____________

Practice 3.3

Subtract to Compare

Use cubes.
Complete the number sentence.

1. 5 (shaded cube)
8 (white cube)

How many fewer (shaded cube) are there?

8 – ____ = ____

2. 7 (white cube)
5 (shaded cube)

How many more (white cube) are there?

____ – ____ = ____

3. 9 (shaded cube)
3 (white cube)

How many more (shaded cube) are there?

____ – ____ = ____

4. 6 (white cube)
11 (shaded cube)

How many fewer (white cube) are there?

____ – ____ = ____

5. 5 (white cube)
13 (shaded cube)

How many fewer (white cube) are there?

____ – ____ = ____

6. 15 (shaded cube)
7 (white cube)

How many more (shaded cube) are there?

____ – ____ = ____

Test Prep

Fill in the ○ for the correct answer. NH means Not Here.

7. Solve.

6 (shaded cube)
9 (white cube)

How many fewer (shaded cube) are there?

2	3	6	NH
○	○	○	○

Explain how you got your answer by writing the number sentence you used.

Name ______________________ Date ____________

Practice 3.4

Use Addition to Subtract

Add or subtract.

Remember
Related facts use the same three numbers.

1. 3
   7

   3 + 7 = 10

   ____ − 7 = 3

2. 4
   5

   4 + 5 = ____

   ____ − 5 = ____

3. 7 + 7 = ____ 14 − 7 = ____	4. 6 + 9 = ____ 15 − 9 = ____	5. 7 + 3 = ____ 10 − 3 = ____
6. 2 + 8 = ____ 10 − ____ = 2	7. 5 + 4 = ____ ____ − 4 = 5	8. 7 + 9 = ____ 16 − 9 = ____
9. 3 + 3 = ____ ____ − 3 = 3	10. 8 + 7 = ____ 15 − ____ = 8	11. 6 + 7 = ____ 13 − ____ =

Test Prep

Fill in the ○ for the correct answer. NH means Not Here.

12. 5 + 9 = 14

    14 − 9 = ____

14	9	5	NH
○	○	○	○

Name ______________________ Date ____________

Practice 3.5

Number Expressions

Write names for the number.

The sums and the differences should equal the number shown.

1. 12   6 + 6   16 − 4   7 + 5

2. 10   ___ − ___   ___ + ___   ___ + ___

3. 6   ___ − ___   ___ + ___   ___ + ___

4. 7   ___ − ___   ___ + ___   ___ − ___

5. 9   ___ + ___   ___ + ___   ___ − ___

6. 3   ___ − ___   ___ − ___   ___ + ___

Test Prep

Fill in the ○ for the correct answer. NH means Not Here.

7. Which of these is not a name for 6.

3 + 3	8 − 2	5 + 2	NH
○	○	○	○

Use with text pages 61–62.

Name ______________________ Date ____________

Practice 3.6

Fact Families

Complete the number sentences.

Remember
A fact family has the same two parts and the same whole.

1. 8 + 3 = 11 3 + 8 = 11 11 − 3 = 8 11 − 8 = 3	2. ____ + 7 = 16 ____ + 9 = 16 ____ − 9 = 7 16 − ____ = 9	3. 2 + 6 = ____ ____ + 2 = 8 ____ − 2 = 6 8 − 6 = ____
4. 9 + ____ = 17 8 + ____ = 17 17 − 9 = ____ 17 − 8 = ____	5. 6 + 8 = ____ ____ + 6 = 14 14 − ____ = 8 14 − ____ = 6	6. ____ + 4 = 11 4 + 7 = ____ 11 − ____ = 4 11 − ____ = 7

Test Prep

Fill in the ○ for the correct answer. NH means Not Here.

7. Which set of numbers makes up the fact family?

9 + 5 = ☐   5 + 9 = ☐

14 − 9 = ☐   14 − 5 = ☐

14 9 9	14 5 5	5 9 14	NH
○	○	○	○

Name ______________________ Date ____________

Practice 3.7

Variables

Find the missing number.

Remember
A fact family has the same two parts and the same whole.

1. __?__ + 7 = 16
   16 − 7 = 9
2. 15 − __?__ = 8
   15 − 8 = ___
3. 6 + __?__ = 10
   10 − 6 = ___
4. 6 + __?__ = 13
   13 − 6 = ___
5. __?__ + 4 = 9
   9 − 4 = ___
6. 8 + __?__ = 17
   17 − 8 = ___
7. 8 + __?__ = 16
   16 − 8 = ___
8. __?__ + 8 = 15
   15 − 8 = ___
9. 3 + __?__ = 12
   12 − 3 = ___
10. 6 + ☐ = 10
    10 − 6 = ___
11. ☐ + 5 = 11
    11 − 5 = ___
12. ☐ + 4 = 9
    9 − 4 = ___

Test Prep

Fill in the O for the correct answer. NH means Not Here.

13. Find the missing number.

8 + ☐ = 14

14 − 8 = __?__

14	8	6	NH
O	O	O	O

Use with text pages 65–66.

Name ______________________________ Date ______________

Problem Solving
Write a Number Sentence

Write a number sentence to solve.

Draw or write to explain.

1. 9 girls and 8 boys twirl streamers in the parade. How many children twirl streamers in the parade?

   _____ children

2. There are 8 children marching in the jazz band. 3 of them play trumpets. How many children play other instruments?

   _____ play other instruments

3. 17 children dance with umbrellas in the parade. 8 umbrellas are yellow. The others are pink. How many umbrellas are pink?

   _____ pink umbrellas

Test Prep

Fill in the ○ for the correct answer. NH means Not Here.

4. Choose the number sentence.

   There are 9 children in the drum band. 4 children play congas. How many children play other kinds of drums?

9 − 7 =	9 + 4 =	9 − 4 =	NH
○	○	○	○

Name ______________________ Date ____________

Practice 4.1

Activity: Take a Survey

Sarah took a survey of her classmates.
Tim took a survey of his classmates.

Sarah's Class

Favorite color	Tally Marks
Blue	|||
Red	卌
Green	|
Orange	
Yellow	||

Tim's Class

Favorite color	Tally Marks
Blue	||||
Red	卌 |
Green	
Orange	||
Yellow	||

Use the data in the charts to answer the questions.

1. Which color is the favorite in both classes?

   red

2. In whose class did more children choose blue?

   ____

3. Which color is liked by the same number of children?

   ____

4. Which color is liked by the fewest children?

   ____

5. How many children altogether like red?

   ______________ children

6. How many children did Tim survey?

   ____

Test Prep

Fill in the ○ for the correct answer. NH means Not Here.

7. Which tally shows 6 children were surveyed?

卌 |   NH

○   

Name ______________________ Date ____________

Practice 4.2

Read a Pictograph

The table shows what games the children like to play during recess.

Simon Says	Jump rope	Catch	Soccer
4	8	6	12

1. Use the table to make a pictograph.

   Draw 1  for every 2 children.

Recess Games

Simon Says	☺ ☺
Jump rope	☺ ☺ ☺ ☺
Catch	☺ ☺ ☺
Soccer	☺ ☺ ☺ ☺ ☺ ☺

Each ☺ stands for 2 children.

Use the information in the pictograph to answer the questions.

2. How many more children like playing soccer than Simon Says?

   _____ more children

3. If 4 more children say they like playing catch best, how many ☺ will you add to the pictograph?

   _____ ☺

Test Prep

Fill in the ○ for the correct answer. NH means Not Here.

4. Each ☆ stands for 2 children.

   What number does 3 ☆ stand for?

8	6	3	NH
○	○	○	○

Name ______________________ Date ____________

Practice 4.3

Activity: Make and Read Bar Graphs

Make a bar graph from the data below.

Miguel sells school supplies. He sold 1 backpack. He sold 2 more books than backpacks. He sold 4 more T-shirts than backpacks.

1.

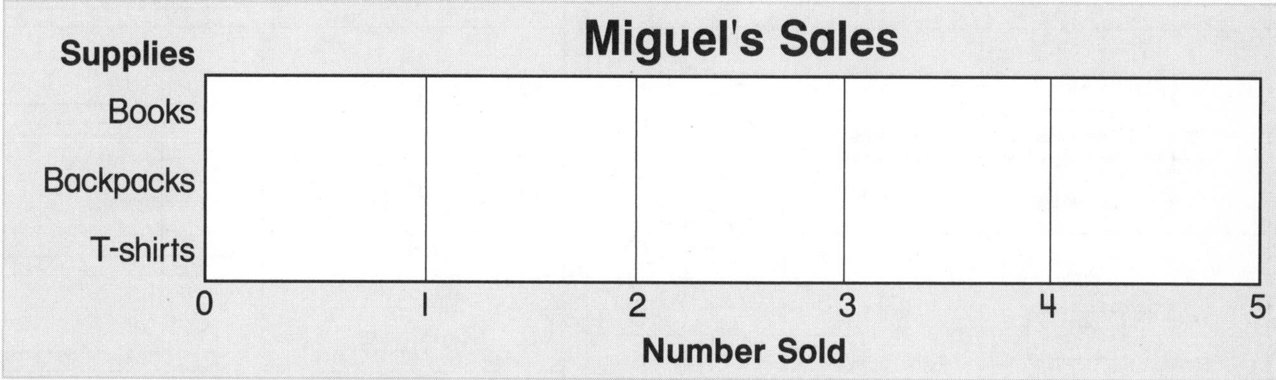

Use the data in the graph to answer the questions.

2. How many books did Miguel sell?

_____

3. How many T-shirts did Miguel sell?

_____

4. What did Miguel sell the fewest of?

____

5. What is the total number of school supplies Miguel sold?

_____

Test Prep

Fill in the ○ for the correct answer. NH means Not Here.

6. Each colored box on a bar graph stands for 2 children. How many boxes must be colored to show 6 children?

8	6	3	NH
○	○	○	○

Name ______________________ Date ______________

Graphing on a Coordinate Grid

Find each place on the grid. Write the ordered pair.

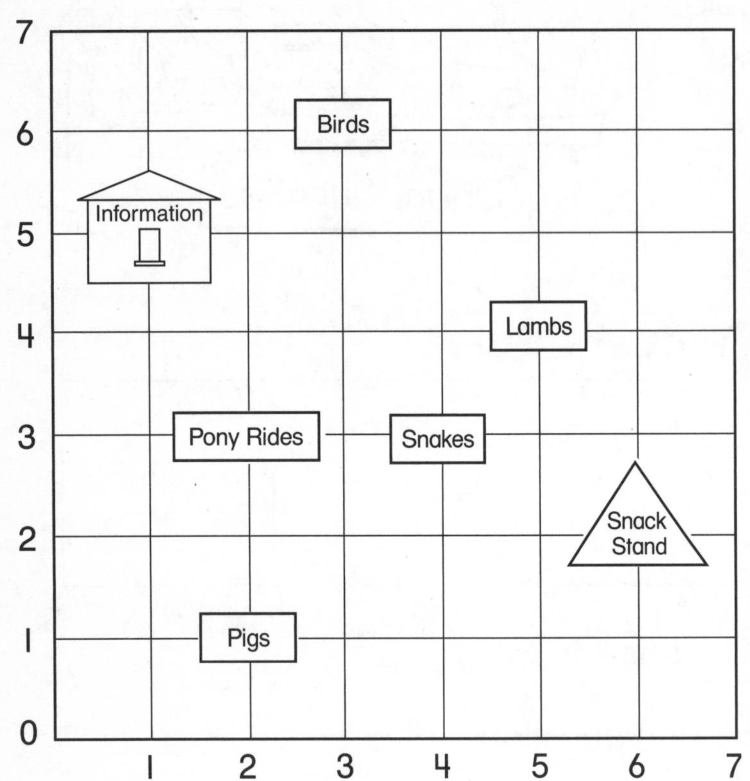

5, 4 means move 5 spaces to the right. Then move 4 spaces up.

Place	Ordered pair
1. Lambs	5, 4
2. Birds	____, ____
3. Information Booth	____, ____
4. Snakes	____, ____
5. Pigs	____, ____

6. If you stopped at point (6, 2), what place would you have visited?

____

Test Prep

Fill in the ○ for the correct answer. NH means Not Here.

7. On a grid, point 1, 4 is located ____ of point 5, 4.

left	right	below	NH
○	○	○	○

Name ________________________________ Date ______________

Range and Mode

Use the data to answer the questions.

The mode is the number that appears most often.
The range is the difference between the largest and smallest number.

How Many Cousins	Number of Children
1	𝍸𝍷
2	𝍷𝍷𝍷𝍷
3	𝍸𝍷𝍷
4	𝍷
5	𝍷𝍷

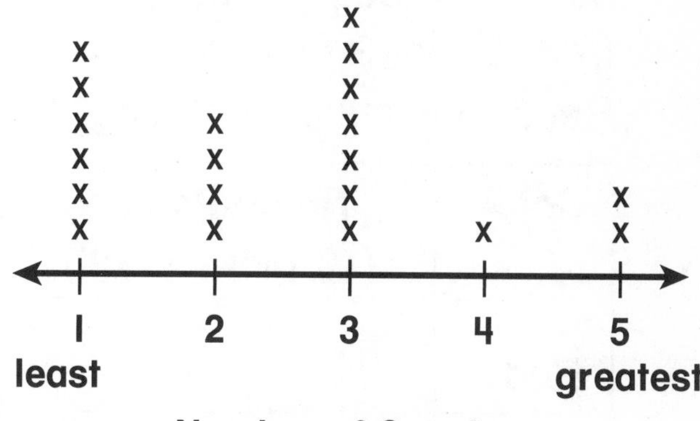

Number of Cousins

1. How many children have 4 cousins?

   _____ child

2. How many children have 2 cousins?

   _____ children

3. How many children have 1 cousin?

   _____ children

4. What is the difference between the greatest number of cousins and the least number of cousins children have?

   _____ − _____ = _____
   greatest least range

Test Prep

Fill in the ○ for the correct answer. NH means Not Here.

5. Three children score 10 on a test. Two children score 9. Five children score 8. What is the mode?

   8 ○ 9 ○ 10 ○ NH ○

Name ______________________ Date ____________

Practice 4.6

Activity: More Likely, Less Likely, Equally Likely

You can compare if an event is more likely, less likely, or equally likely to happen.

1. Place 7 red cubes and 5 blue cubes in a bag. Pick one cube from a bag. Record the color. Return the cube to the bag.

Color	Times Picked (10 picks in all)
Red	
Blue	

How likely are you to pick a red cube rather than a blue cube?

more likely   less likely   equally likely

2. Place 3 red cubes and 9 blue cubes in a bag. Pick one cube from a bag. Record the color. Return the cube to the bag.

Color	Times Picked (10 picks in all)
Red	
Blue	

How likely are you to pick a red cube rather than a blue cube?

more likely   less likely   equally likely

3. Which event is probable? Circle.

I will choose a .

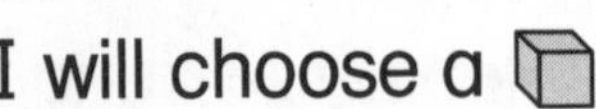

I will choose a .

4. Which event is impossible? Circle.

I will choose a .

I will choose a .

Test Prep

Fill in the ○ for the correct answer. NH means Not Here.

5. An event that is equally likely to happen is _____.

impossible	probable	certain	NH
○	○	○	○

Name ______________________ Date ____________

Practice 4.7

Activity: Predicting Outcomes

When you predict the outcome of an event, you tell what will most likely happen.

1. Predict the color the spinner will land on most often. white

Use a paper clip and pencil. Spin 15 times. Record your spins.

Color	Tally	Tally
White		
Gray		
Black		

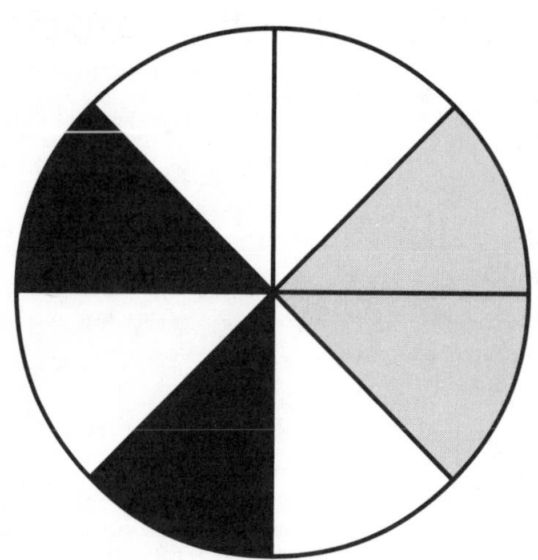

2. Which color did you land on most often?

____

____

3. Draw a large circle. Draw lines to mark parts of the circle. Use three colors to color the parts. Use blue to color the part the spinner would land on most often.

Test Prep

Fill in the ○ for the correct answer. NH means Not Here.

4. May spins a spinner 10 times. The spinner is half blue and half orange. How many times do you predict she will spin orange?

10	5	3	NH
○	○	○	○

Name ______________________ Date ____________

Practice 4.8

Problem Solving Use a Graph

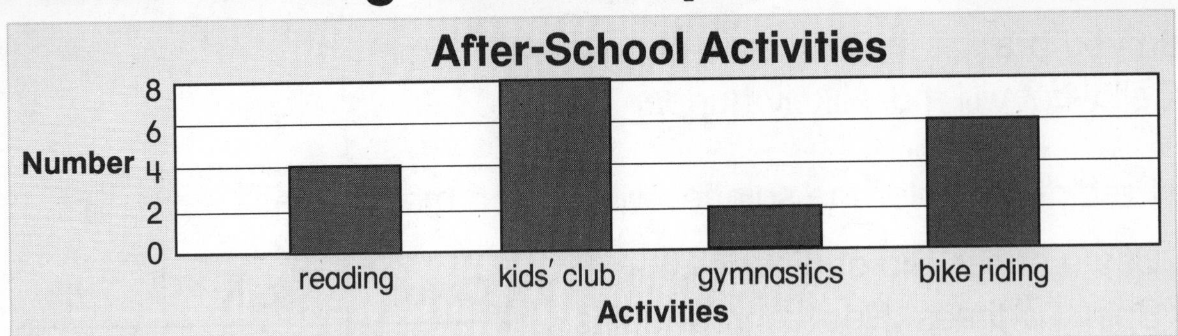

Use the data in the graph to solve.

Draw or write to explain.

1. How many children like to read?

   4 children

2. How many children altogether like bike riding and gymnastics?

   _____ children

3. How many more children like kids' club rather than reading?

   _____ children

4. Which activity do children like least of all?

   ____

Test Prep

Fill in the ○ for the correct answer. NH means Not Here.

5. Justin wants to make a bar graph. He wants to show that 9 children like soccer, 4 children like videos, and 3 children like skating. What number must each box on the graph stand for?

   ○ 4 ○ 2 ○ 1 ○ NH

Use with text pages 99–101.

Name ______________________ Date ____________

Practice 5.1

Tens through 100

Write the number of tens.
Then write the value.

Remember
Think 10 more when you count by tens.

1. 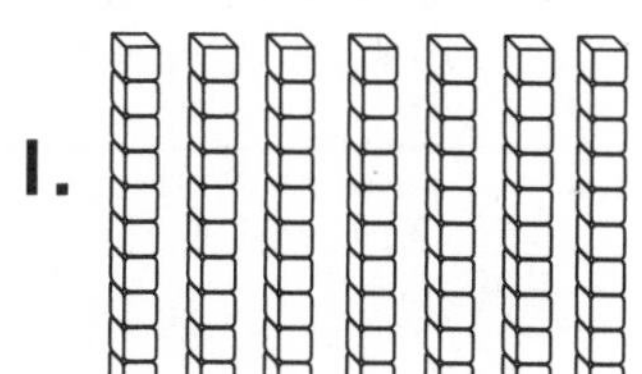

seventy

7 tens

70

2. 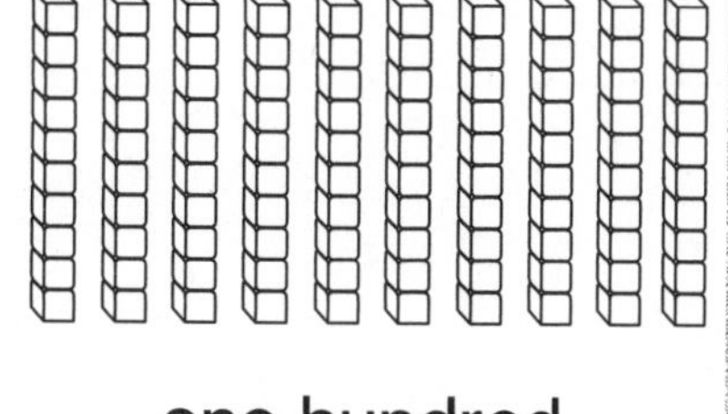

one hundred

_____ tens

_____

3. 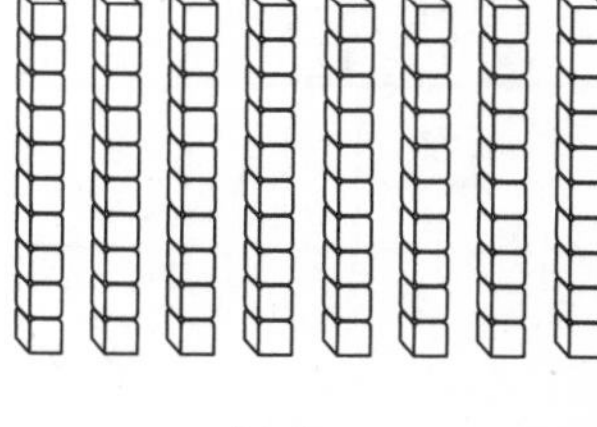

eighty

_____ tens

_____

4. 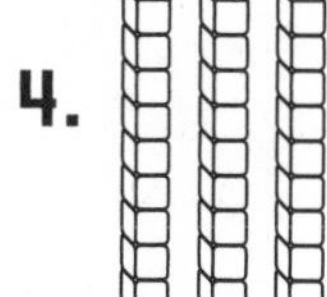

thirty

_____ tens

_____

5. 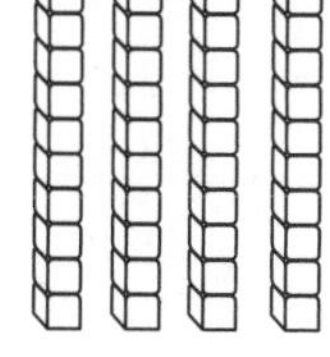

forty

_____ tens

_____

6. 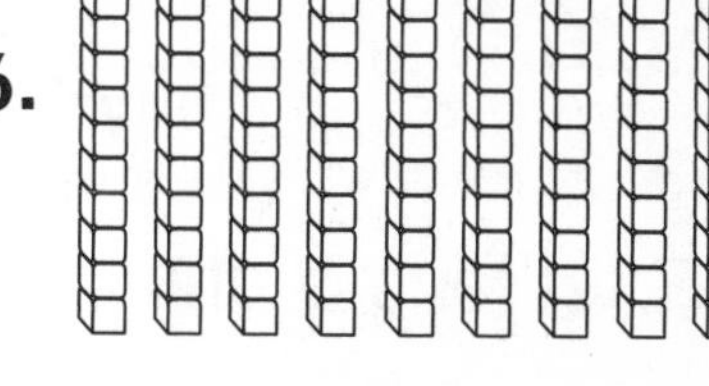

ninety

_____ tens

_____

Write the missing numbers.

7. 10, 20, _____

8. _____, 50, _____

9. 70, _____, _____, _____

Test Prep

Fill in the ○ for the correct answer. NH means Not Here.

10. How many tens are in 50?

50	5	0	NH
○	○	○	○

Name ______________________ Date ______________

Practice 5.2

Tens and Ones to 100

Write the tens and ones.

1. 4 tens 5 ones

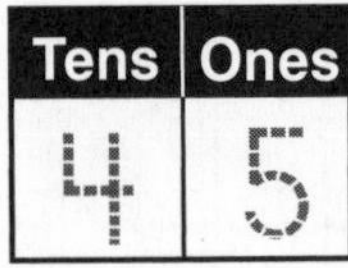

Tens	Ones
4	5

45

forty-five

2. 9 tens 2 ones

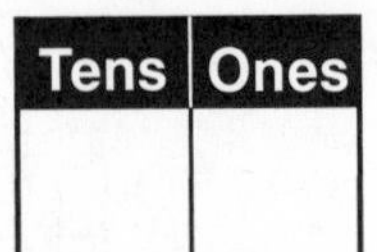

Tens	Ones

______

ninety-two

3. 5 tens 3 ones

Tens	Ones

______

fifty-three

4. 7 tens 0 ones

Tens	Ones

______

seventy

5. 2 tens 6 ones

Tens	Ones

______

twenty-six

6. 1 ten 8 ones

Tens	Ones

______

eighteen

Test Prep

Fill in the ○ for the correct answer. NH means Not Here.

7. Which shows the number in words?

Tens	Ones
8	3

○ eighty-three ○ thirty-eight ○ five ○ NH

Name ______________________ Date __________

Practice 5.3

Identify Place Value

Complete the chart.

Remember
To find the value of a digit, find the value of its place.

Count how many.	Write the tens and ones.	Write the value of each digit.	Write the number.
1.	3 tens 2 ones	___ + ___	___
2.	___ tens ___ ones	___ + ___	___

Circle the value of the darker digit.

3. **6**7
   60 6

4. 9**8**
   80 8

5. **2**3
   20 2

6. 4**4**
   40 4

7. **8**5
   80 8

8. 7**1**
   10 1

Solve.

I have fewer ones than tens. The value of my tens is 30.
What two numbers can I be? ________

Test Prep

Fill in the ○ for the correct answer. NH means Not Here.

9. Which number has the value of 2 tens and 9 ones?

92 ○ 79 ○ 29 ○ NH ○

Name ________________________ Date ____________

Practice 5.4

Different Ways to Make Numbers

Circle two ways to make the number.

1. 68 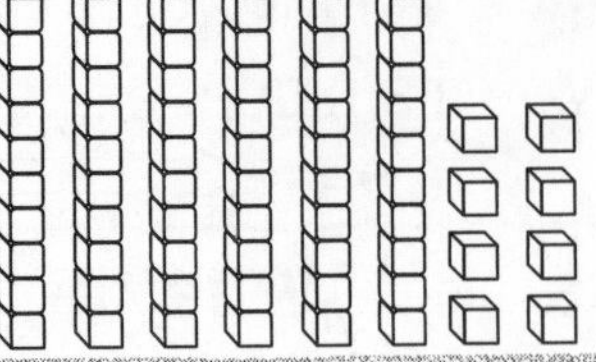 8 tens 6 ones 60 + 8

2. 31 30 + 1 1 ten 3 ones 

3. 57 5 tens 7 ones 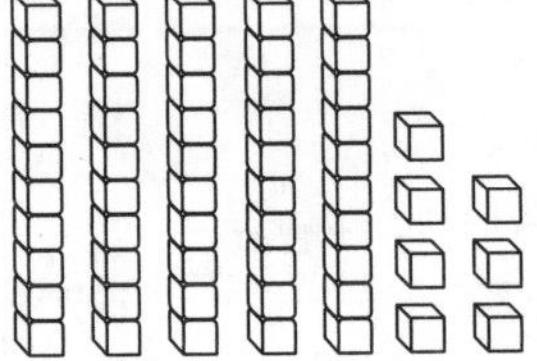 5 + 70

4. 14 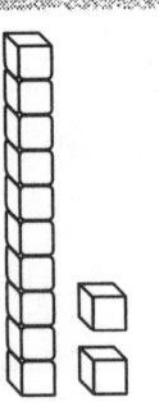 10 + 4 

5. 26 20 + 6 20 + 60 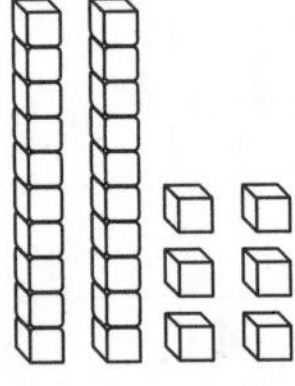

6. 72 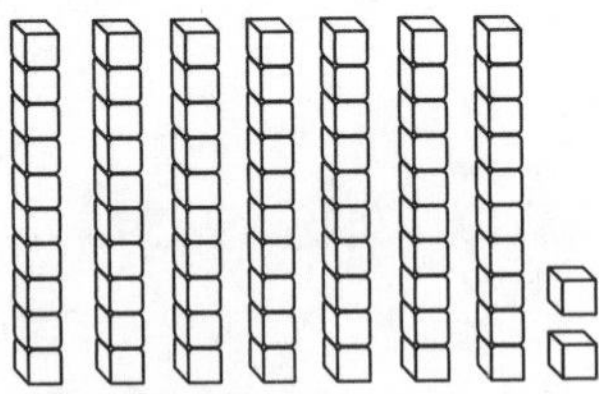 7 tens 2 ones 2 tens 7 ones

Test Prep

Fill in the ○ for the correct answer. NH means Not Here.

7. Which shows another way to make 29?

20 tens 9 ones	2 tens 9 ones	29 tens	NH
○	○	○	○

Name ______________________ Date ______________

Compare Two-Digit Numbers

Remember
First compare the tens.
If you need to, then
compare the ones.

Write >, <, or =.

1. 52 (>) 23	**2.** 81 ○ 96	**3.** 23 ○ 32
4. 32 ○ 12	**5.** 50 ○ 70	**6.** 48 ○ 27
7. 61 ○ 72	**8.** 85 ○ 85	**9.** 94 ○ 99
10. 93 ○ 63	**11.** 30 ○ 39	**12.** 18 ○ 25
13. 52 ○ 52	**14.** 75 ○ 71	**15.** 56 ○ 46
16. 91 ○ 90	**17.** 28 ○ 28	**18.** 45 ○ 54
19. 37 ○ 33	**20.** 65 ○ 64	**21.** 10 ○ 20

Test Prep

Fill in the ○ for the correct answer. NH means Not Here.

22. Compare the numbers. Choose the symbol.

68 ○ 86

>	<	=	NH
○	○	○	○

Name ______________________ Date ____________

Decision: Reasonable Answers

Circle the most reasonable answer.

Draw or write to explain.

1. This year Brad invited 15 friends to a skating party. Last year he invited fewer friends. How many friends did he invite last year?

   12 friends   18 friends   20 friends

2. The Swim Club has 20 children. The Make-a-Mask Club has more children. How many children are in the Make-a-Mask Club?

   16 children   25 children   80 children

3. Tan can juggle 5 balls. Nela can juggle even more. How many balls can Nela juggle?

   3 balls   7 balls   24 balls

Test Prep

Fill in the ○ for the correct answer. NH means Not Here.
Choose the most reasonable answer.

4. Max collects baseball cards. He has 22 cards. He sold 7 of them to get spending money. How many cards does Max have left?

29	20	15	NH
○	○	○	○

Name ______________________ Date ____________

Practice 6.1

Even and Odd Numbers

Use cubes or draw dots.
Make groups of two to show the number.
Circle even or odd.

Remember
Odd numbers have 1, 3, 5, 7, or 9 in the ones place.
Even numbers have 2, 4, 6, 8, or 0 in the ones place.

1. 16 even odd
2. 22 even odd
3. 27 even odd
4. 20 even odd
5. 18 even odd
6. 12 even odd
7. 13 even odd
8. 23 even odd

9. Color the even numbers Red.
Color the odd numbers Blue.

15	16	17	18	19	20

Test Prep

Fill in the ○ for the correct answer. NH means Not Here.

10. Which is an odd number?

8	10	13	NH
○	○	○	○

Name ______________________ Date ____________

Practice 6.2

Activity: Skip Counting

Use the hundred chart.

Remember
When you skip count on a hundred chart, the numbers follow a pattern.

1	2	3	4	5			8		10
11				15	16			19	
	22			25		27	28		
31		33					38		40
	42				46	47		49	
	52		54			57		59	

1. Write the missing numbers.
2. Count by 5s. Circle the numbers.
3. Count by 3s. Put an X on the numbers.

Follow the pattern.
Write the missing numbers.

4. 21, 24, 27, _____, 33, _____

Test Prep

Fill in the ○ for the correct answer. NH means Not Here.

5. Continue the pattern. What is the next number?

34, 38, 42, _____

44	48	52	NH
○	○	○	○

Name ______________________ Date ____________

Practice 6.3

Order Two-Digit Numbers to 100

Use the number line.

Remember
A number line can help you find a number that comes just before, between, or just after.

Write the number that comes just after.

1. 72, 73, 74
2. 81, 82, ____
3. 78, 79, ____

Write the number that comes just before.

4. ____, 78, 79
5. ____, 81, 82
6. ____, 71, 72

Write the number that comes between.

7. 88, ____, 90
8. 77, ____, 79
9. 85, ____, 87

Write the missing numbers.

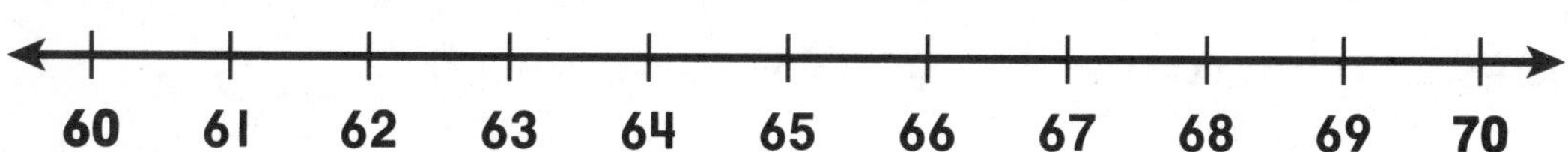

10. 69, 68, ____, 66, ____, 64, ____, 62, 61

11. What number is just after 69? ____

Test Prep

Fill in the ○ for the correct answer. NH means Not Here.

12. What number comes between 76 and 78?

75 ○ 77 ○ 79 ○ NH ○

Name ______________________ Date ____________

Practice 6.4

Ordinal Numbers

You use ordinal numbers to tell where people or things are. Use the picture. Circle the answer.

1. Which step is below the twelfth step?

 13th 11th 12th

2. Which step is above the 18th step?

 eighteenth seventeenth nineteenth

3. Which step is between the fourteenth step and the sixteenth step?

 15th 17th 13th

4. Which step is just above the bottom step?

 twentieth second nineteenth

5. Which step is just before the last step?

 19th 20th 1st

 Test Prep

Fill in the ○ for the correct answer. NH means Not Here.

6. How many steps are between the eighth step and the eleventh step?

1	2	3	NH
○	○	○	○

Name ______________________ Date ______________

Practice 6.5

Repeating and Growing Patterns

Draw the next picture to continue the pattern.
Write the numbers.

1.

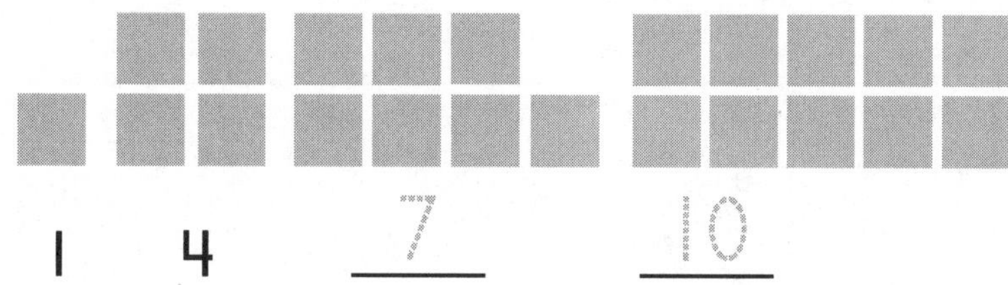

1 4 7 10 13

2.

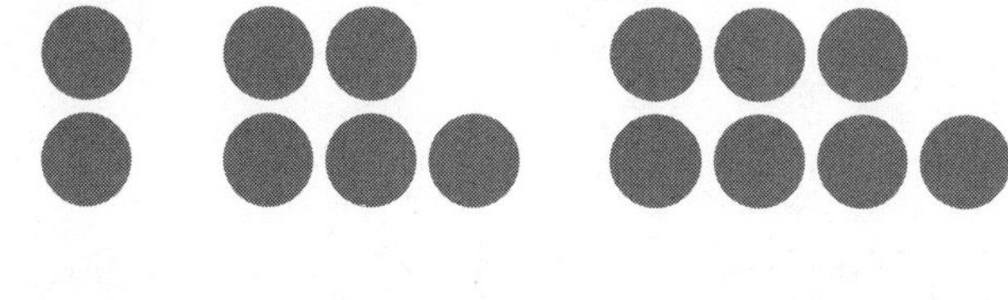

____ ____ ____ ____

3. 8, 4, 6, 8, 4, 6, 8, 4, 6, ____

4. 15, 25, 35, 45, 55, ____, ____

5. 24, 26, 28, 30, 32, ____, ____

Test Prep

Fill in the ○ for the correct answer. NH means Not Here.

6. Which letter pattern is like the number pattern
123, 123, 123?

AB	ABC	AA	NH
○	○	○	○

Name ______________________ Date ______________

Practice 6.6

Problem Solving Find a Pattern

Look for the pattern. Then solve.

Draw or write to explain.

1. There are 2 horses to pull each cart. How many horses pull 5 carts?

Wagons	1	2	3	4	5
Horses	2	4	6	8	10

______ horses pull 5 wagons.

2. Each clown has 4 balloons. How many balloons do 6 clowns have?

Clowns	1	2	3	4	5	6
Balloons	4	8				

______ balloons

3. There are 5 acrobats in each row. How many acrobats are in 7 rows?

Rows	1	2	3	4	5	6	7
Acrobats	5	10	15				

______ acrobats

Test Prep

Fill in the ○ for the correct answer. NH means Not Here.

4. Find the pattern. Solve.

Each clown has 3 hats in a bag.
How many hats are in 4 bags?

6	9	12	NH
○	○	○	○

Name ______________________ Date ______________

Plane Shapes

Circle the shape that matches the name.

1. rectangle

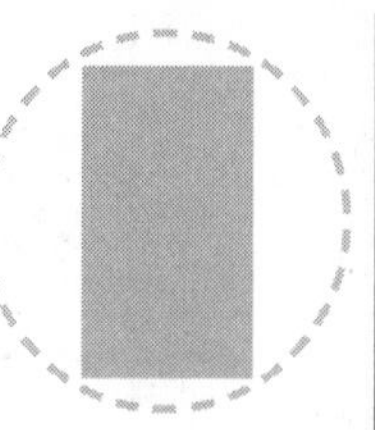

2. square

3. hexagon

4. circle

5. trapezoid

6. triangle

Write the name of the shape.

7.  ______________

8.  ______________

9.  ______________

10.  ______________

Test Prep

Fill in the ○ for the correct answer. NH means Not Here.

11. Name the shape.

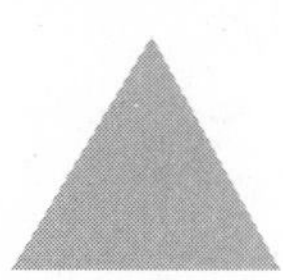

hexagon	rectangle	triangle	NH
○	○	○	○

Name ______________________ Date ______________

Practice 7.2

Sides and Vertices

Match the objects and the sentences.

1. It has 0 sides.

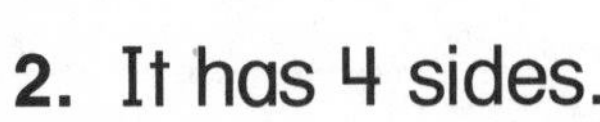

2. It has 4 sides.

3. It has 3 sides.

Write the name of the shape.
Write two reasons for your answer.

square

rectangle

circle

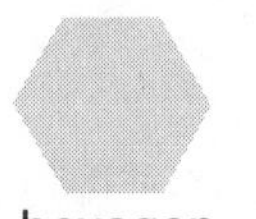
hexagon

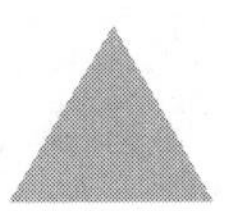
triangle

trapezoid

4.

____

____

____

5.

____

____

____

Test Prep

Fill in the ○ for the correct answer. NH means Not Here.

6. Which shape has four sides that are the same?

triangle	rectangle	square	NH
○	○	○	○

Name ______________________ Date ____________

Practice 7.3

Congruent Shapes

Circle the shape that is congruent to the first shape.

Remember
Congruent shapes are the same size and shape.

1\.

2\.

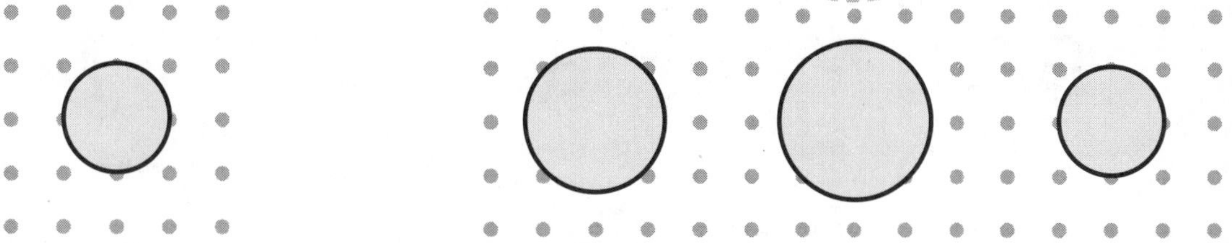

3\.

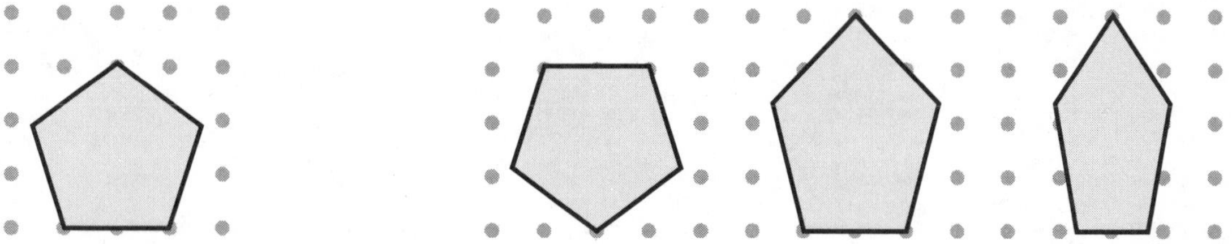

4\.

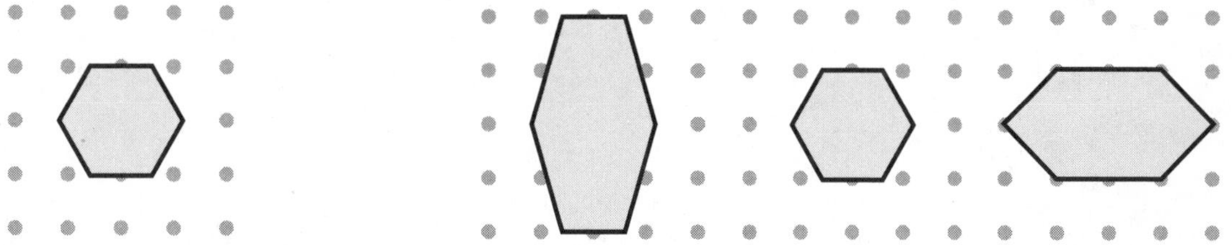

Fill in the ○ for the correct answer. NH means Not Here.

5\. Which shape is congruent to the triangle?

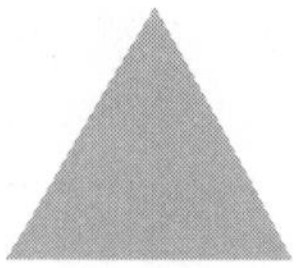

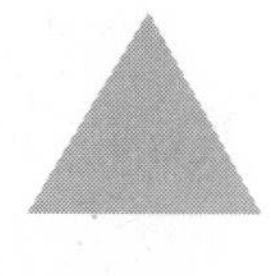

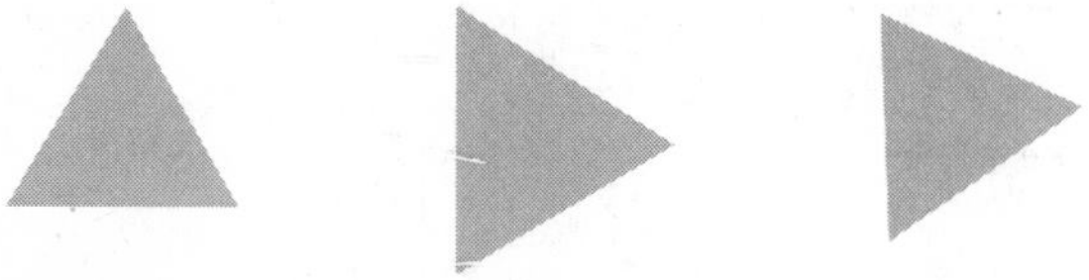

○

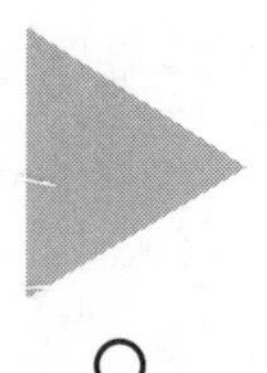

○

○

NH

○

Use with text pages 187–188.

Name ______________________ Date ____________

Practice 7.4

Symmetry

Circle the shape if it has a line of symmetry.
Draw the line.

1. W	2. 5	3. V
4. F	5. 3	6. M
7. 9	8. H	9. O
10. D	11. 7	12. X

Test Prep

Fill in the ○ for the correct answer. NH means Not Here.

13. Which shape shows a correctly drawn line of symmetry?

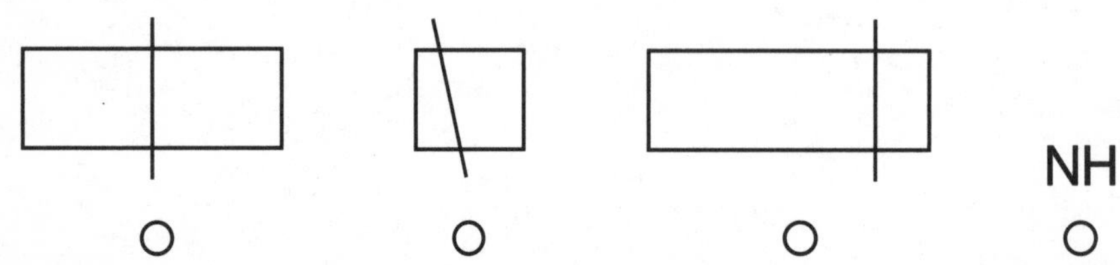

Name ______________________ Date ____________

Practice 7.5

Combine and Separate Shapes

Use the blocks. Make Shape A. Trace the blocks.
Then, make a new shape. Trace the blocks.

	Use these blocks.	Shape A	New Shape
1.	2 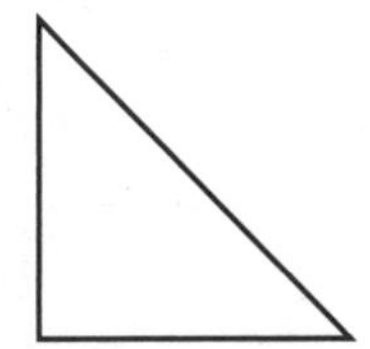	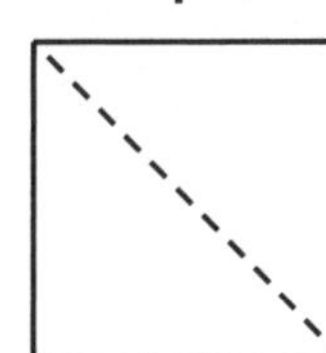	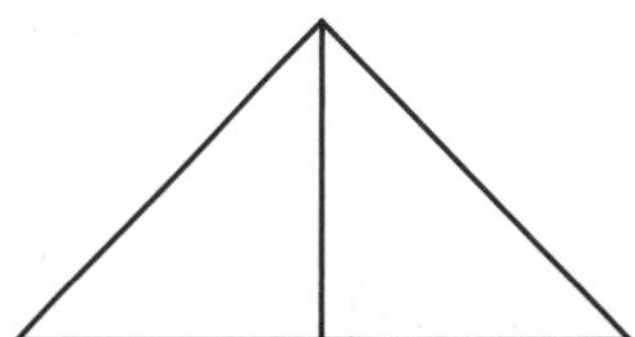
2.	3, 1 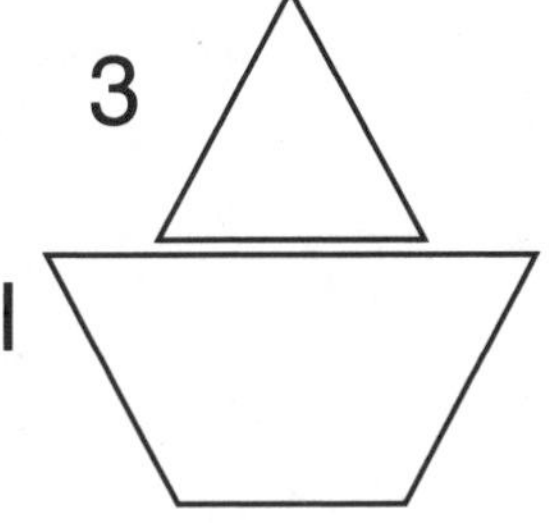		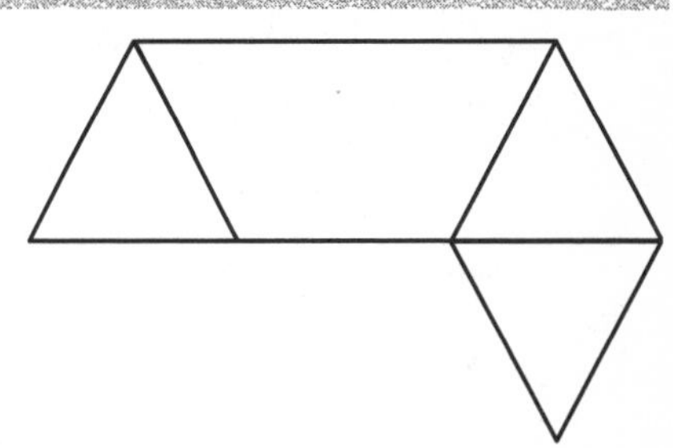
3.	4, 1 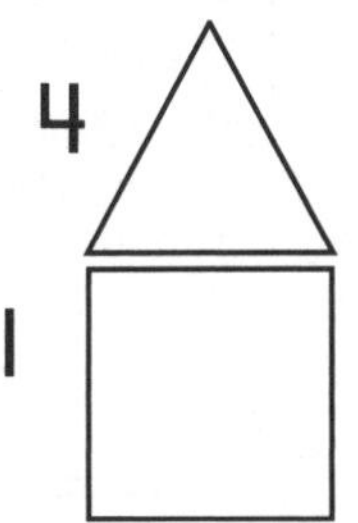	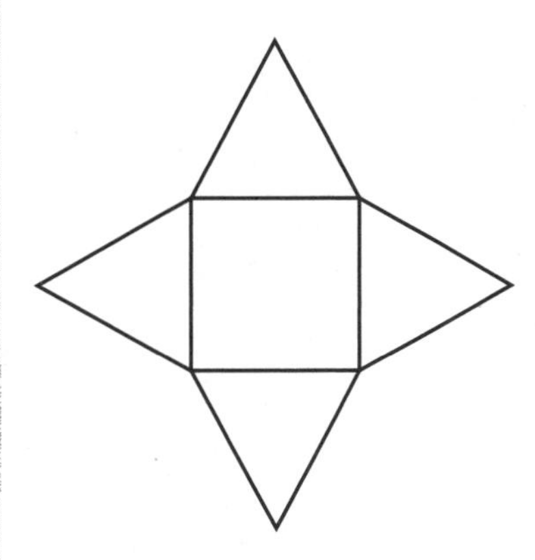	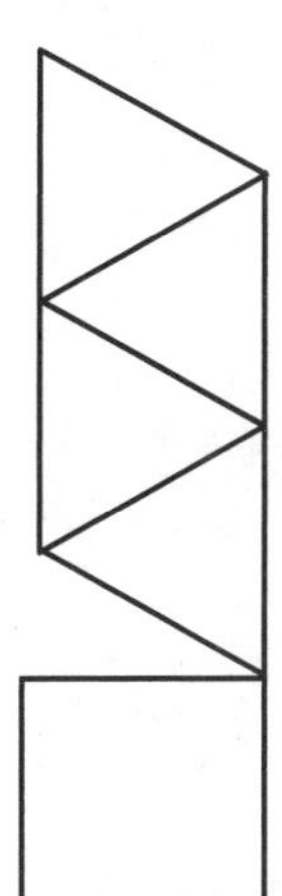

Test Prep

Fill in the ○ for the correct answer. NH means Not Here.

4. What shape can you make with 2 ?

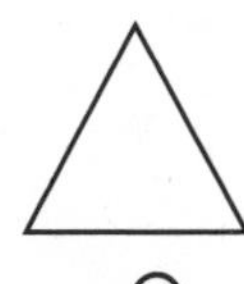 ○ 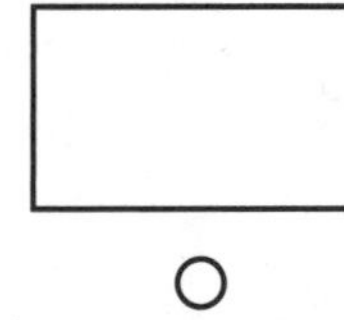 ○ 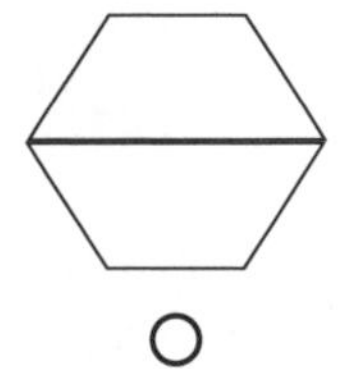 ○  NH ○

Name ______________________ Date ____________

Practice 7.6

Slides, Flips, and Turns

Look at the shape.
Write slide, flip, or turn.

Remember
You can move shapes in different ways.

1.

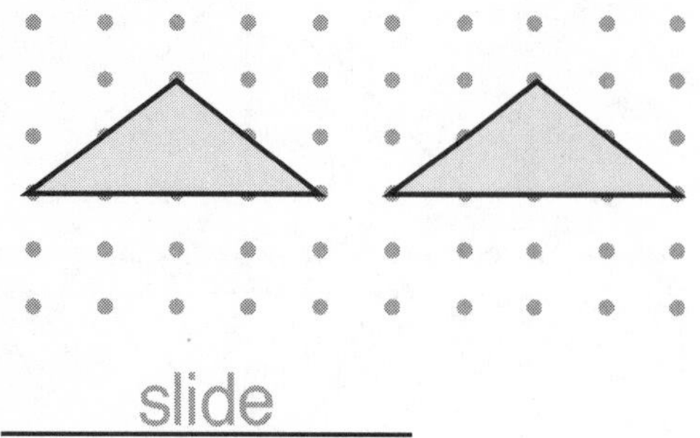

slide

2.

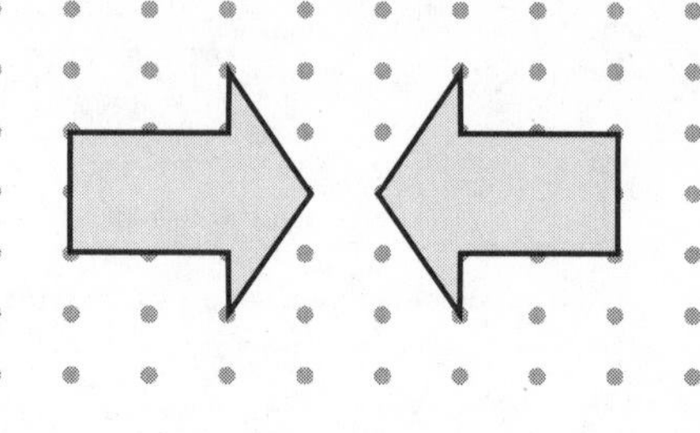

____

3.

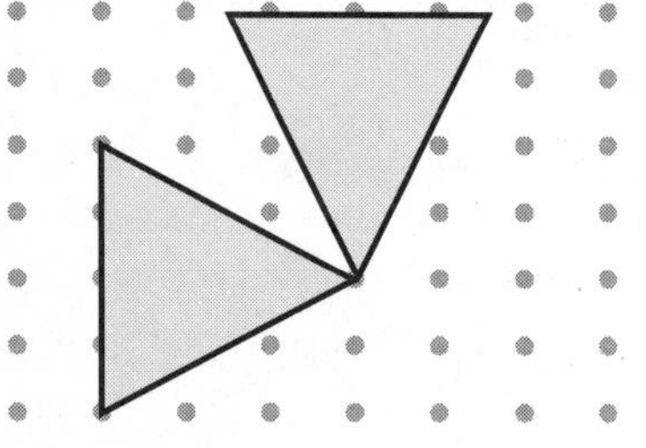

____

4.

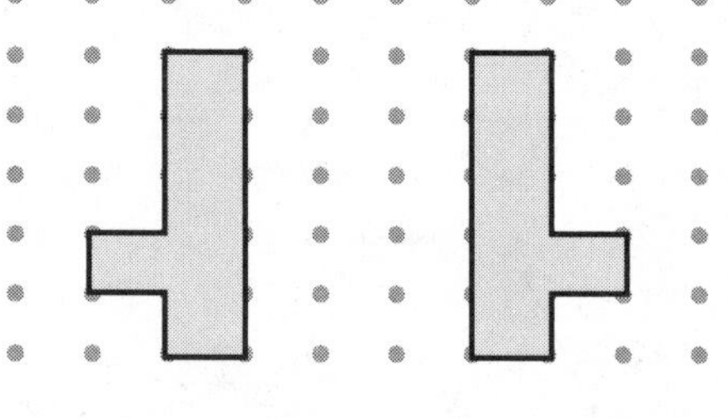

____

Test Prep

Fill in the ○ for the correct answer.
NH means Not Here.

5. Which shape shows a slide?

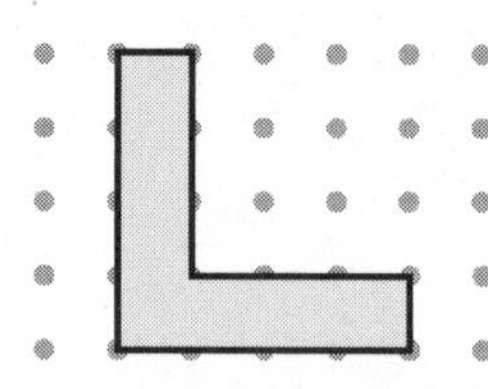

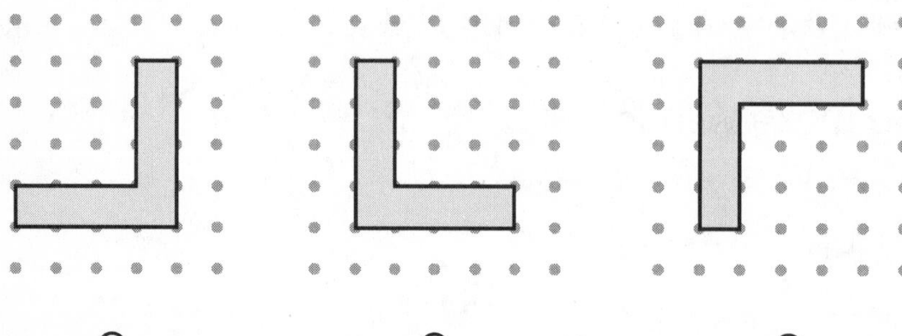

○ ○ ○ NH ○

Name ______________________ Date ____________

Practice 7.7

Problem Solving Find a Pattern

Look for the pattern.

Draw or write to explain.

1. Lucy drew a pattern on a birthday card she was making. What two shapes are likely to come next?

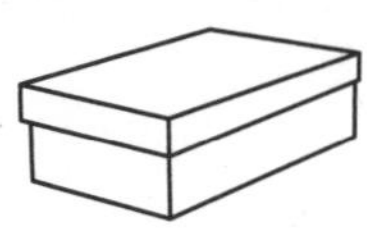 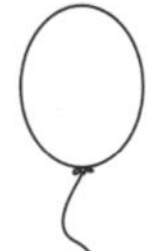  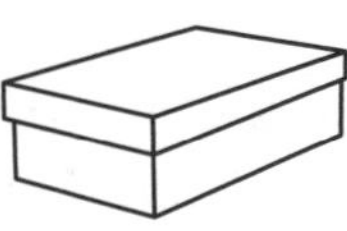

______________ ______________

2. Ben is making a border for his poster. What two shapes are likely to come next?

______________ ______________

3. Millie is making some wrapping paper with a pattern. Here is the beginning of the pattern: a shape with four equal sides, a shape with three sides and a point at the top, a shape with no sides at all. How is the pattern likely to continue?

__________ __________ __________

Test Prep

Fill in the ○ for the correct answer. NH means Not Here.

4. What two shapes are likely to come next?
XXOMXXOMXX _____

MM	XO	OM	NH
○	○	○	○

Name ______________________ Date ____________

Practice 8.1

Identifying Solid Shapes

  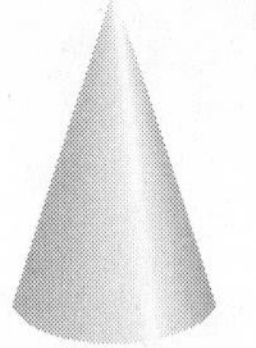 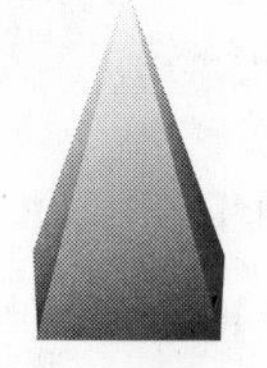  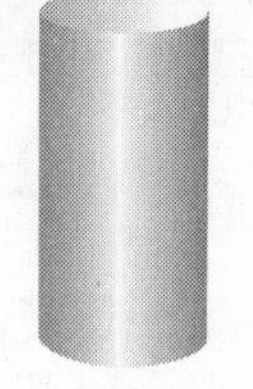

cube	sphere	cone	square pyramid	rectangular prism	cylinder

Write the names of the two solid shapes in the picture.

1\.

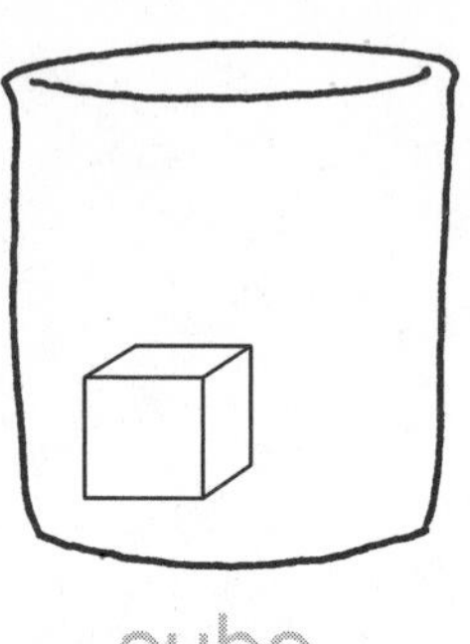

cube

cylinder

2\.

____

____

3\.

____

____

4\.

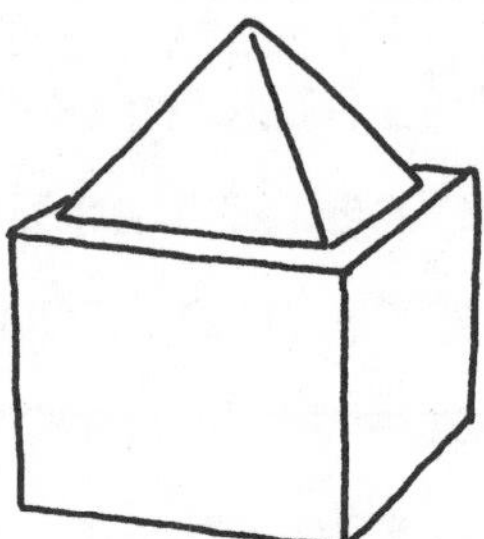

____

____

Test Prep

Fill in the ○ for the correct answer. NH means Not Here.

5\. Which object is an example of a cylinder?

ice-cream cone	soup can	cereal box	NH
○	○	○	○

Use with text pages 207–208.

Name ______________________ Date ____________

Faces, Edges, and Vertices

Circle the shapes that match the number of faces, edges, and vertices.

1. 6 faces, 12 edges, 8 vertices

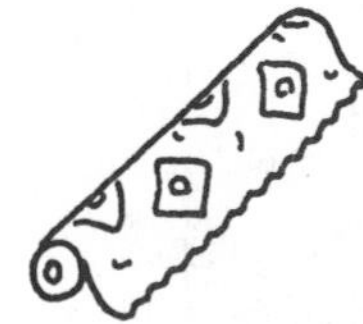

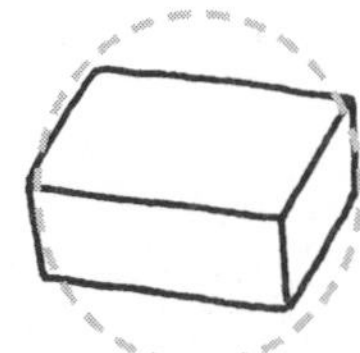

2. 1 face, 0 edge, 0 vertex

3. 0 faces, 0 edges, 0 vertices

4. 6 faces, 12 edges, 8 vertices

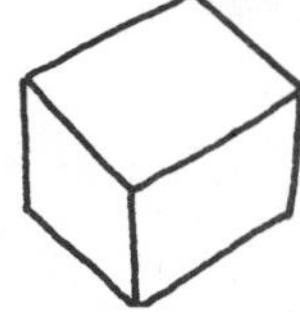

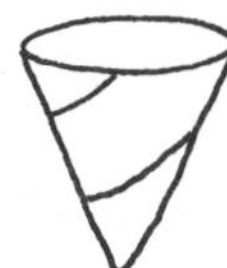

5. 2 faces, 0 edges, 0 vertices

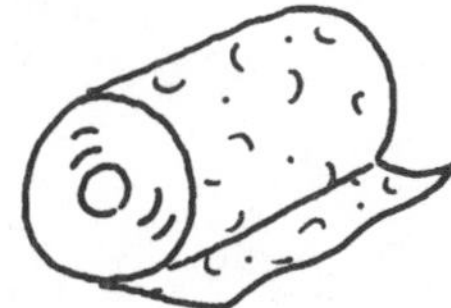

Test Prep

Fill in the ○ for the correct answer. NH means Not Here.

6. Which solid does not roll?

cone	sphere	square pyramid	NH
○	○	○	○

Name ______________________ Date ____________

Practice 8.3

Activity: Plane Shapes on Solid Shapes

Draw the picture of the plane shapes you would make if you traced the faces on the solid shapes.

1. 

2. 

3. 

4.  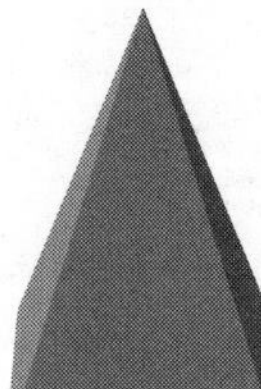

Test Prep

Fill in the ○ for the correct answer. NH means Not Here.

5. Which solid shape will give you a circle when you trace a face?

cylinder	rectangular prism	sphere	NH
○	○	○	○

Use with text pages 211–212.

Name ______________________ Date ____________

Practice 8.4

Classify and Compare Solid Shapes

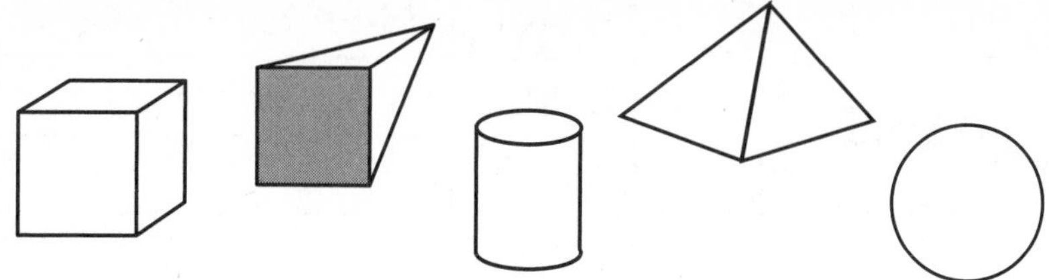

Remember
Count faces, edges, and vertices to compare solid shapes.

Write how the pair is alike or different.

	Alike	Different
1.	Both shapes have a square face.	A cube has 6 square faces; a square pyramid has 1 square face.
2.		
3.		

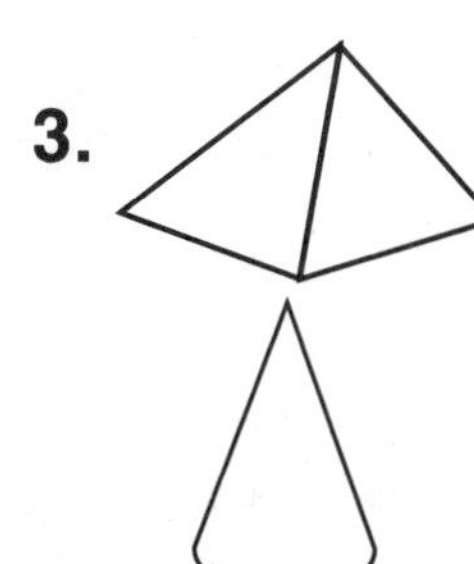

Test Prep

Fill in the ○ for the correct answer. NH means Not Here.

4. Which shape does not roll or stack?

square pyramid ○ cube ○ cone ○ NH ○

Name ______________________ Date ____________

Practice 8.5

Problem Solving
Use Logical Thinking

Each member of the team got to vote for a team color. Look at the results of the vote.

Color	Number of Votes
blue	14
red	11
green	7
black	2

Use the table. Solve.

Draw or write to explain.

1. Anna chose the color that got more votes than green. Her color got an odd number of votes. Which color did Anna choose?

   ____

2. Daryl likes the color that got more than 2 votes. His color got an even number of votes. Which color did Daryl choose?

   ____

3. Sarah chose the color that got fewer than 14 votes. Her color got an even number of votes. Which color did Sarah choose? ____________

Test Prep

Fill in the ○ for the correct answer. NH means Not Here.

4. 14 children want a frog for a class pet. 3 more children than that want a snake. 2 fewer children than the snake group want a rabbit. How many children want a rabbit?

19	17	15	NH
○	○	○	○

Name ______________________ Date ____________

Practice 9.1

Unit Fractions

Write the fraction for the shaded part.

1. 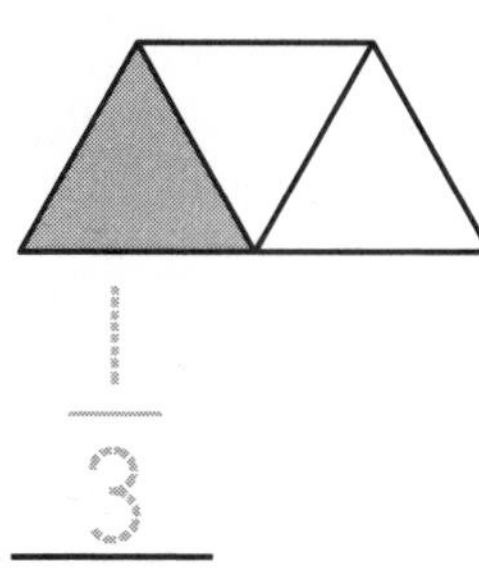

2. 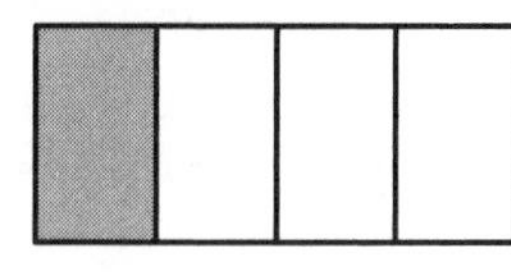

______

3. 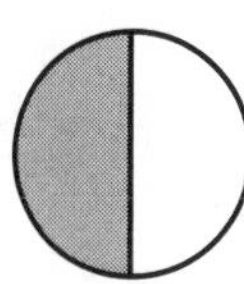

______

4. 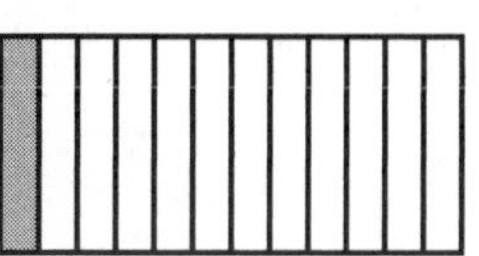

______

5. 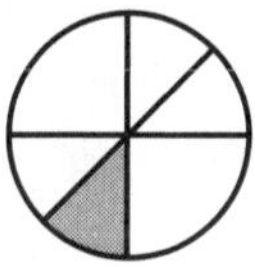

______

6. 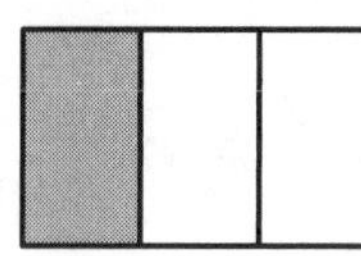

______

Color to show one shaded part.

7. 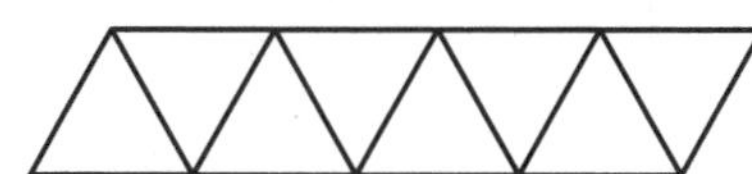

$\frac{1}{8}$

8. 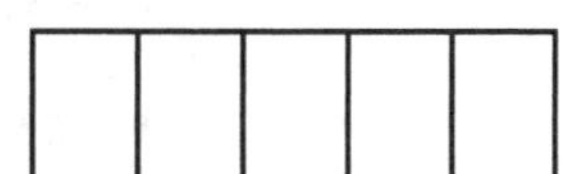

$\frac{1}{5}$

9. 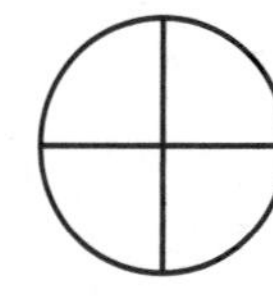

$\frac{1}{4}$

Test Prep

Fill in the ○ for the correct answer. NH means Not Here.

10. What is the fraction for the shaded part?

$\frac{1}{3}$	$\frac{1}{2}$	$\frac{1}{4}$	NH
○	○	○	○

Name ______________________ Date ____________

Practice 9.2

Other Fractions

Write the fraction for the shaded parts.

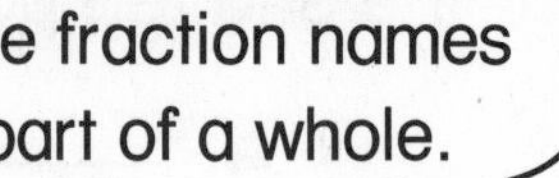

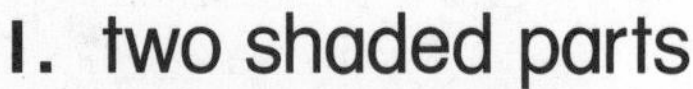

1. two shaded parts

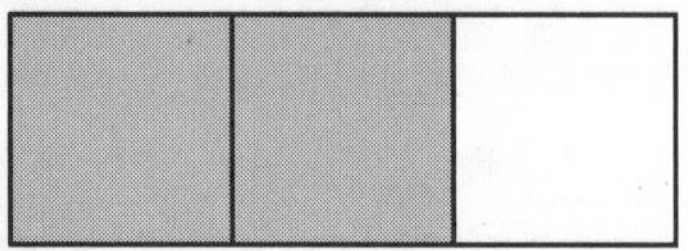

$\frac{2}{3}$

2. one shaded part

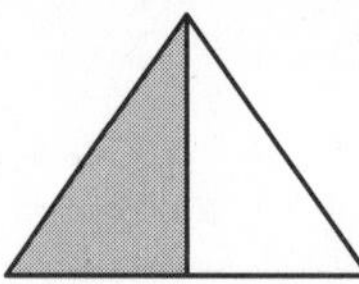

______

3. four shaded parts

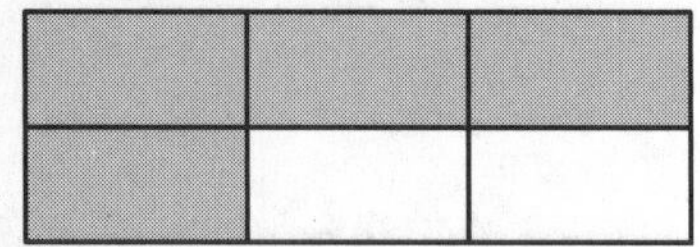

______

4. seven shaded parts

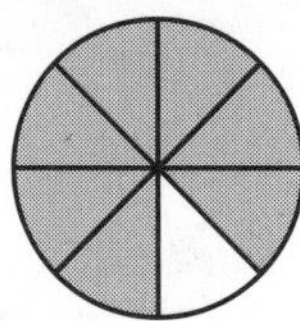

______

Color to show the number of shaded parts.
Write the fraction for the shaded parts.

5. three shaded parts

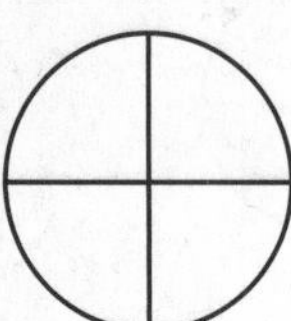

______

6. six shaded parts

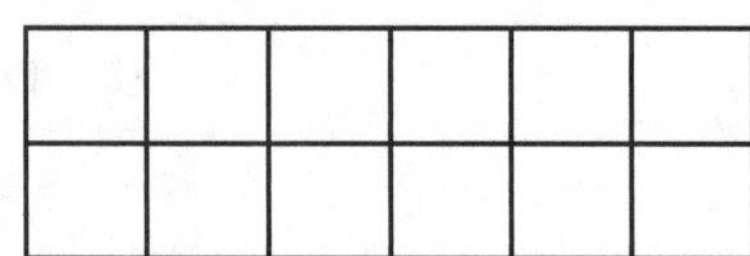

______

7. four shaded parts

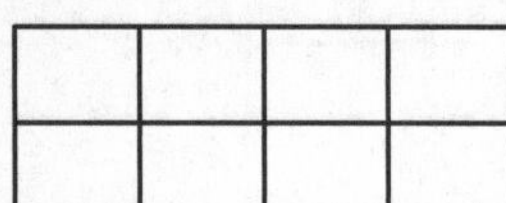

______

8. three shaded parts

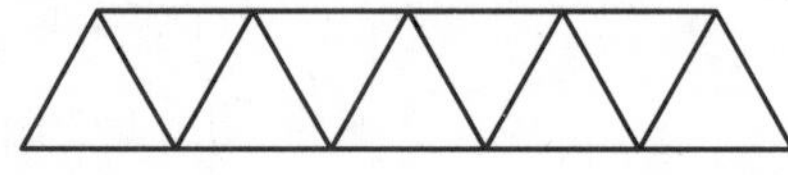

______

Test Prep

Fill in the ○ for the correct answer. NH means Not Here.

9. How many parts does this shape show?

5	4	3	NH
○	○	○	○

Name ______________________ Date ____________

Practice 9.3

Wholes and Parts

Write the fraction for the shaded parts.

1. 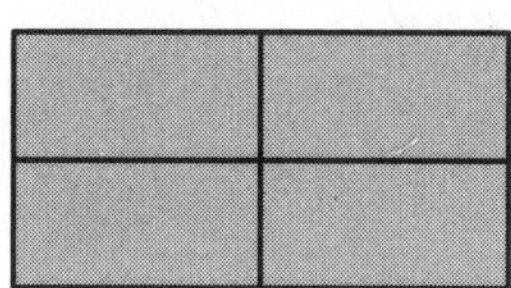

$\frac{4}{4}$

2. 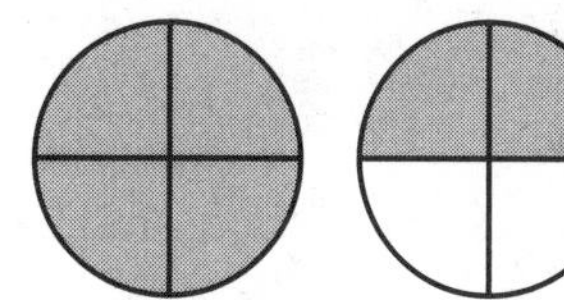

____

3. 

____

4. 

____

5. 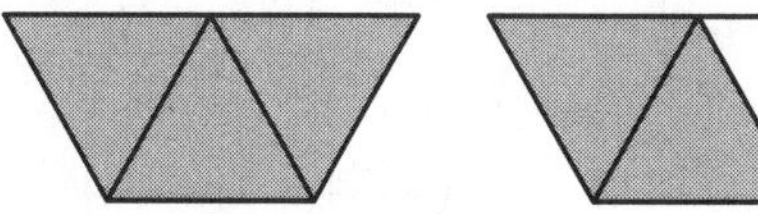

____

6. 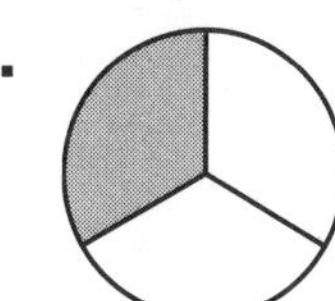

____

Test Prep

Fill in the ○ for the correct answer. NH means Not Here.

7. What fraction does this shape show?

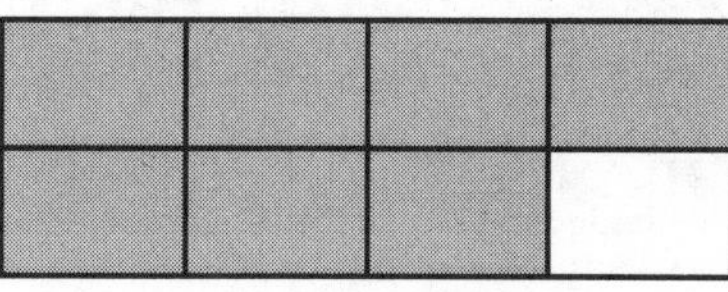

$\frac{4}{8}$ ○ $\frac{6}{8}$ ○ $\frac{7}{8}$ ○ NH ○

Use with text pages 231–232.

Name ______________________ Date ____________

Practice 9.4

Comparing Fractions

Compare the shaded parts.
Write > or <.

Remember
\> is greater than
and
< is less than.

1. 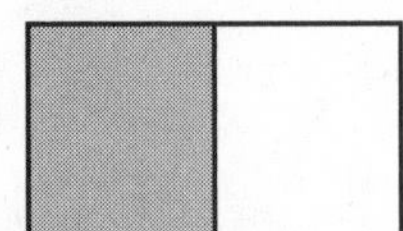 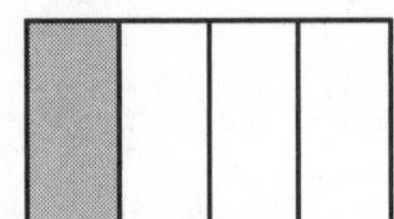

$\frac{1}{2}$ (>) $\frac{1}{4}$

2. 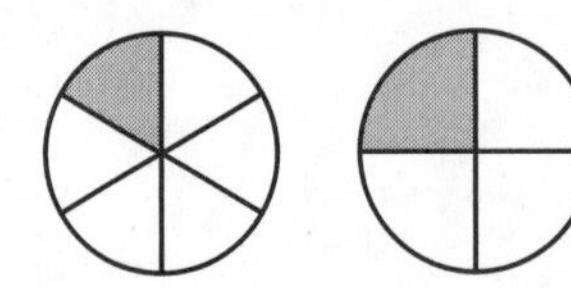

$\frac{1}{6}$ ◯ $\frac{1}{4}$

3. 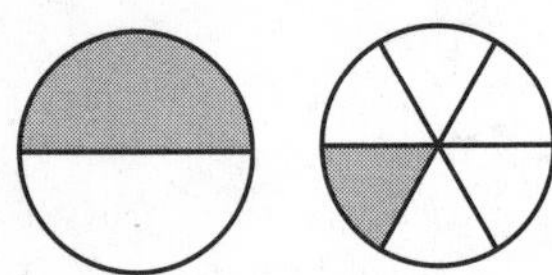

$\frac{1}{2}$ ◯ $\frac{1}{6}$

4.  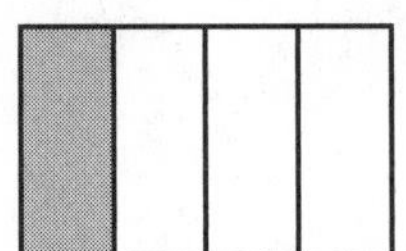

$\frac{1}{8}$ ◯ $\frac{1}{4}$

5. 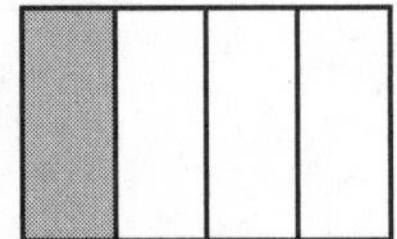 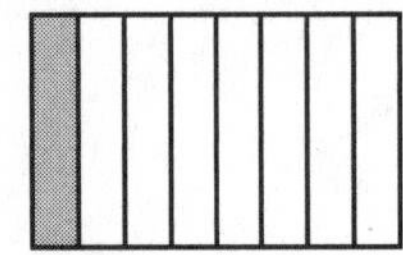

$\frac{1}{4}$ ◯ $\frac{1}{8}$

6. 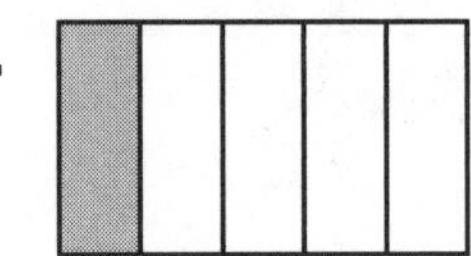 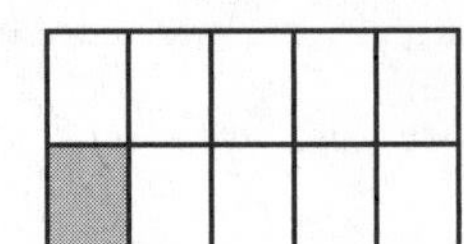

$\frac{1}{5}$ ◯ $\frac{1}{10}$

Test Prep

Fill in the ○ for the correct answer. NH means Not Here.

7. Compare. Choose the symbol.

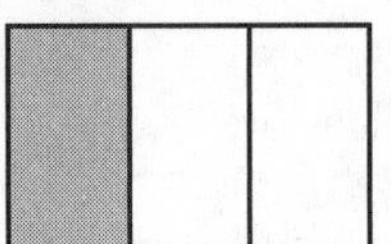 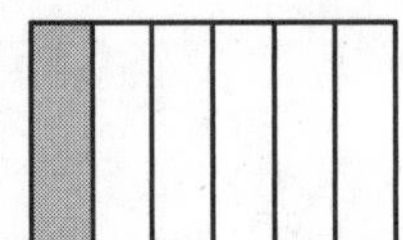

$\frac{1}{3}$ ◯ $\frac{1}{6}$

>	<	=	NH
○	○	○	○

Name ____________________ Date ____________

Practice 9.5

Fractions of a Set

Write a fraction for each color.

1. 

$\frac{3}{6}$ black $\frac{3}{6}$ gray

2. 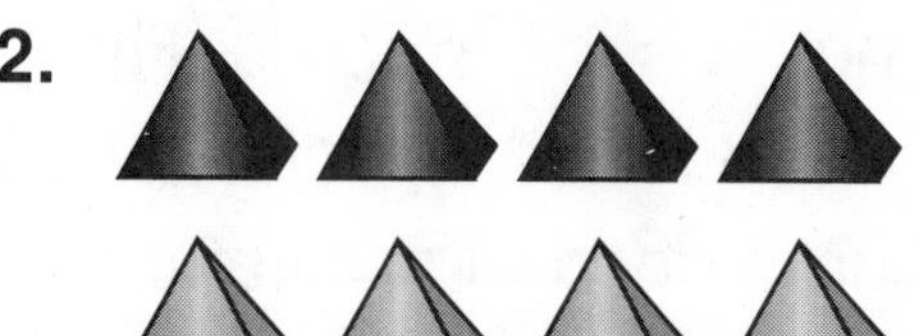

____ black ____ gray

3. 

____ black ____ gray

4. 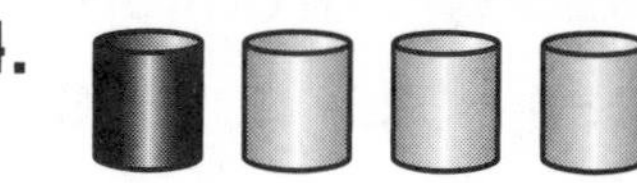

____ black ____ gray

5. 

____ black ____ gray

6. 

____ black ____ gray

Test Prep

Fill in the ○ for the correct answer. NH means Not Here.

7. What is one fraction these colors show?

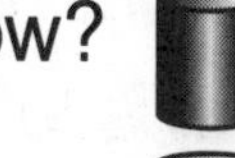

$\frac{2}{8}$ ○ $\frac{3}{8}$ ○ $\frac{4}{8}$ ○ NH ○

Name ______________________ Date ____________

Problem Solving Use a Picture

Use the picture to solve the problem.

1. Max has 6 soccer cards. He gives 4 to Rosie. What fraction of the cards does Max give to Rosie?

   $\frac{4}{6}$ of the cards

2. Patsy has 4 shells. She gives 1 shell to Lewis. What fraction of the shells does Patsy have left?

   ____ of the shells

3. Benjamin brings 12 oranges to baseball practice. The team eats 6 oranges. What fraction of oranges does the team eat?

   ____ of the oranges

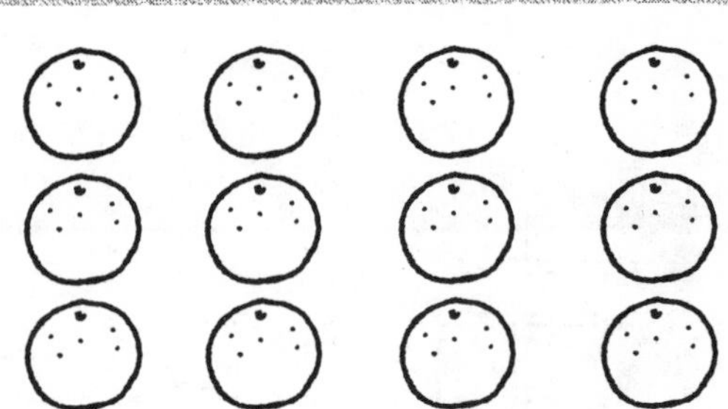

Test Prep

Fill in the ○ for the correct answer. NH means Not Here.

4. Use the picture. Solve.

   Mrs. Wells cut an apple pie into 8 pieces. The children eat 6 pieces. What fraction of the pie is left?

$\frac{6}{8}$	$\frac{4}{8}$	$\frac{2}{8}$	NH
○	○	○	○

Name ______________________ Date ____________

Practice 10.1

Mental Math: Add Tens

Remember
Think about addition facts.

Complete the addition sentences.

1. 2 tens + 6 tens = 8 tens
   20 + 60 = 80

2. 5 tens + 3 tens = ____ tens
   ____ + ____ = ____

3. 3 tens + 4 tens = ____ tens
   ____ + ____ = ____

4. 1 ten + 1 ten = ____ tens
   ____ + ____ = ____

5. 7 tens + 1 ten = ____ tens
   ____ + ____ = ____

6. 3 tens + 6 tens = ____ tens
   ____ + ____ = ____

7. 4 tens + 2 tens = ____ tens
   ____ + ____ = ____

8. 1 ten + 8 tens = ____ tens
   ____ + ____ = ____

9. 2 tens + 7 tens = ____ tens
   ____ + ____ = ____

10. 2 tens + 2 tens = ____ tens
    ____ + ____ = ____

Test Prep

Fill in the ○ for the correct answer. NH means Not Here.

11. What is the missing number?

1 ten + ____ tens = 5 tens

4	3	2	NH
○	○	○	○

Name ______________________ Date ____________

Practice 10.2

Count on Tens to Add

Use the hundred chart.
Add.

1. 27 + 30 = 57

2. 10 + 16 = ______

3. 43 + 30 = ______

4. 50 + 21 = ______

5. 82 + 10 = ______

6. 60 + 25 = ______

1	2	3	4	5	6	7	8	9	10
11	12	13	14	15	16	17	18	19	20
21	22	23	24	25	26	27	28	29	30
31	32	33	34	35	36	37	38	39	40
41	42	43	44	45	46	47	48	49	50
51	52	53	54	55	56	57	58	59	60
61	62	63	64	65	66	67	68	69	70
71	72	73	74	75	76	77	78	79	80
81	82	83	84	85	86	87	88	89	90
91	92	93	94	95	96	97	98	99	100

7. 11 + 40

8. 20 + 32

9. 79 + 10

10. 50 + 14

11. 10 + 57

12. 40 + 51

13. 62 + 10

14. 30 + 31

Test Prep

Fill in the ○ for the correct answer. NH means Not Here.

15. What is the missing number?

17 + ____ = 47

○ 20 ○ 40 ○ 60 ○ NH

Name ______________________ Date __________

Practice 10.3

Regroup Ones as Tens

Use Workmat 3 with [ten rod] and [unit cube].
Write the tens and ones.
Regroup. Write the number.

Remember
Regroup
10 ones as 1 ten.

1. 3 tens 15 ones [45] Regroup → 4 tens 5 ones [45]

Regroup. Write the number.

2. 6 tens 10 ones Regroup → ____ tens ____ ones [ ]

3. 5 tens 14 ones Regroup → ____ tens ____ ones [ ]

4. 1 ten 19 ones Regroup → ____ tens ____ ones [ ]

5. 7 tens 13 ones Regroup → ____ tens ____ ones [ ]

6. 2 tens 11 ones Regroup → ____ tens ____ one [ ]

Test Prep

Fill in the ○ for the correct answer. NH means Not Here.

7. How many tens are there after you regroup 2 tens and 18 ones?

3	2	1	NH
○	○	○	○

Name _______________ Date _______________

Practice 10.4

Decide When to Regroup

Use Workmat 3 with [tens block] and [ones cube].

Remember
Regroup when there are 10 or more ones.

Show both numbers.	Add the ones. How many tens and ones are there?	Do you need to regroup?	What is the sum?
1. 24 + 6	2 tens 10 ones	(Yes) No	30
2. 51 + 4	____ tens ____ ones	Yes No	
3. 47 + 5	____ tens ____ ones	Yes No	
4. 63 + 7	____ tens ____ ones	Yes No	
5. 38 + 6	____ tens ____ ones	Yes No	
6. 59 + 7	____ tens ____ ones	Yes No	
7. 26 + 3	____ tens ____ ones	Yes No	
8. 38 + 9	____ tens ____ ones	Yes No	

Test Prep

Fill in the ○ for the correct answer. NH means Not Here.

9. Which addition sentence needs to have ones regrouped?

16 + 2	10 + 5	12 + 9	NH
○	○	○	○

Name ______________________ Date ____________

Practice 10.5

Add One-Digit Numbers to Two-Digit Numbers

Remember
Regroup when you have ten or more ones.

Use Workmat 3 with [tens] and [ones].

1.
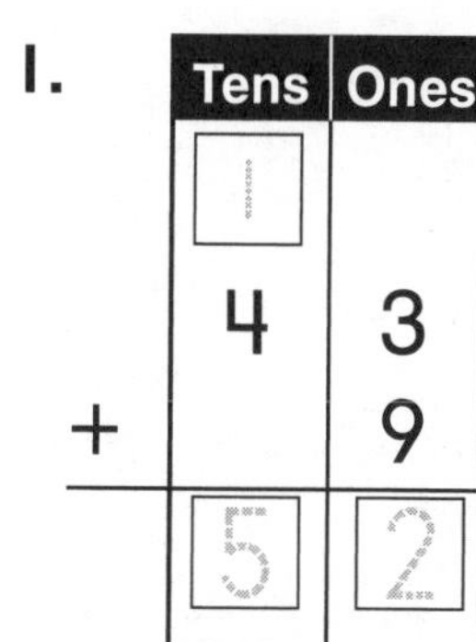

2.

	Tens	Ones
	☐	
	3	8
+		4
	☐	☐

3.
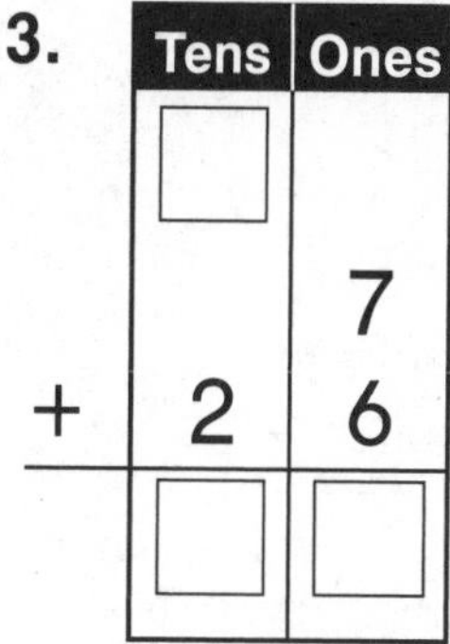

4.
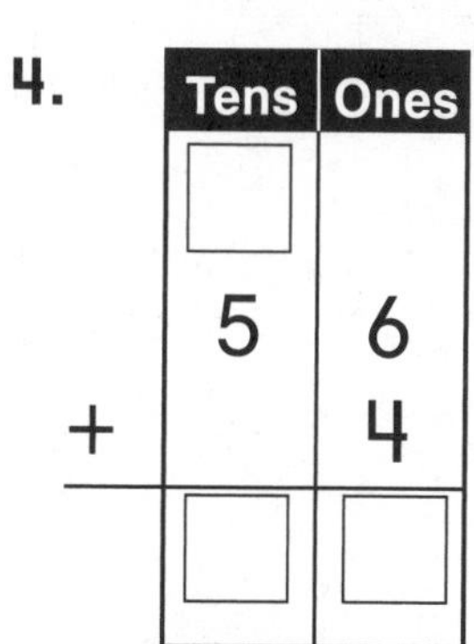

5.

	Tens	Ones
	☐	
		8
+	2	7
	☐	☐

6.
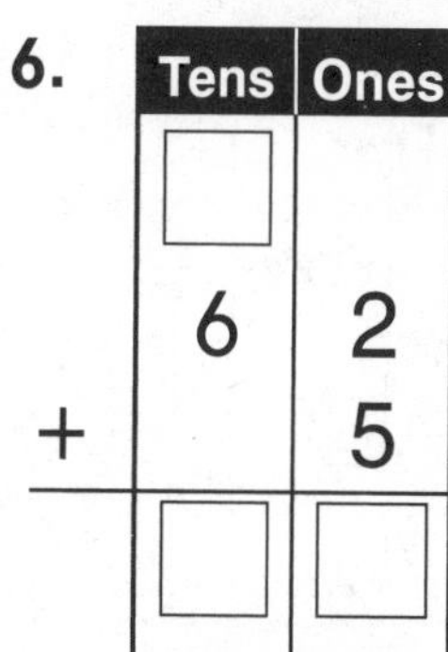

7.

	Tens	Ones
	☐	
	7	0
+		8
	☐	☐

8.

	Tens	Ones
	☐	
	1	5
+		7
	☐	☐

9.
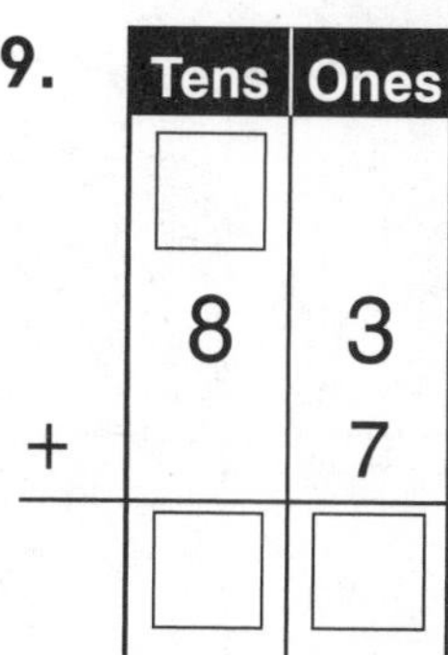

Test Prep

Fill in the ○ for the correct answer. NH means Not Here.

10. When you add 65 + 8, how many ones are in the sum?

13	7	3	NH
○	○	○	○

Name ______________________ Date ______________

Practice 10.6

Add Two-Digit Numbers

Use Workmat 3 with [tens] and [ones].

Remember
When you regroup, record in the tens column.

1.

Tens	Ones
1	
3	6
+ 2	7
6	3

2.

Tens	Ones
	9
+ 3	7

3.

Tens	Ones
4	5
+ 1	5

4.

Tens	Ones
4	7
+ 2	9

5.

Tens	Ones
5	8
+	4

6.

Tens	Ones
2	7
+ 5	2

7.

Tens	Ones
	9
+ 3	8

8.

Tens	Ones
6	3
+ 1	8

9.

Tens	Ones
4	2
+ 3	0

Test Prep

Fill in the ○ for the correct answer. NH means Not Here.

10. Which addition sentence needs regrouping of ones?

38 + 2 ○ 38 + 1 ○ 38 + 0 ○ NH ○

Name ______________________ Date ____________

Practice 10.7

Problem Solving
Too Much Information

Cross out information you do not need. Then solve.

Draw or write to explain.

1. In the park, 14 children play on the slides. 8 are boys and 6 are girls. 20 children play on the climbing tower. How many children play in the park?

   34 children

2. There are 12 children playing running games. 10 others play quiet board games. 3 teachers watch the children. How many children play?

   ______ children

3. 11 children choose raisins as a snack. There are about 30 raisins in each box. The other 9 children want juice. How many children enjoy snacks?

   ______ children

Test Prep

Fill in the ○ for the correct answer. NH means Not Here.
Read and solve.

4. 4 children go to bed early. 6 stay up late to read. 14 others stay up to draw. How many children stay up late?

10	18	20	NH
○	○	○	○

Name ______________________ Date ____________

Practice 11.1

Rewrite to Add

> **Remember**
> When you rewrite the addends, line up the ones.

Rewrite the addends. Add.

1. 16 + 54

	Tens	Ones
	1	
	1	6
+	5	4
	7	0

2. 8 + 29

	Tens	Ones
+		

3. 62 + 33

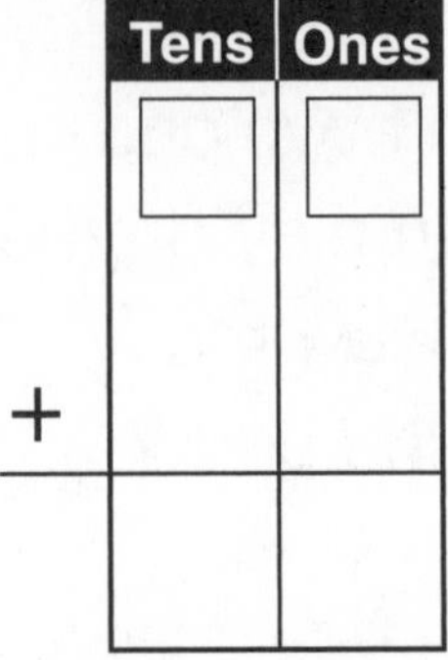

4. 81 + 9

	Tens	Ones
+		

5. 79 + 3

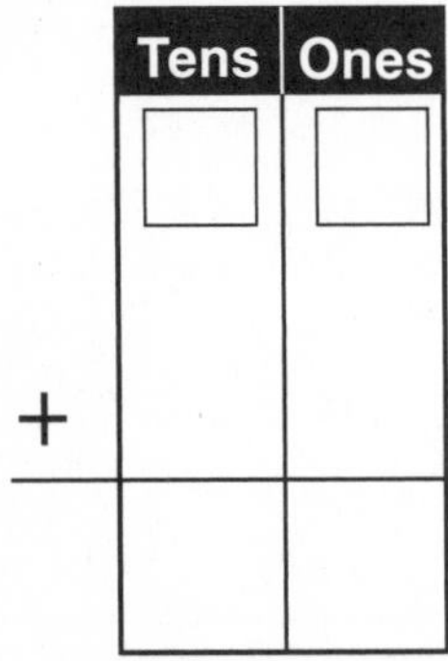

6. 46 + 48

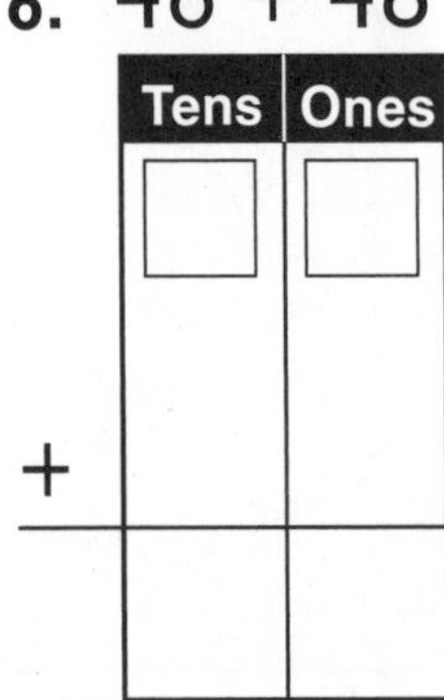

7. 27 + 16

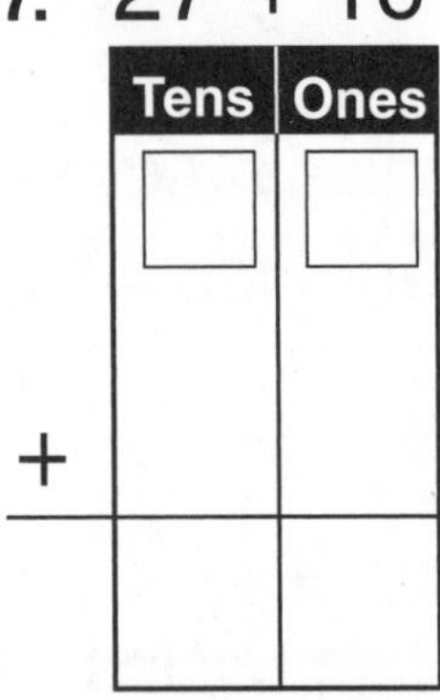

8. 57 + 13

	Tens	Ones
+		

9. 17 + 29

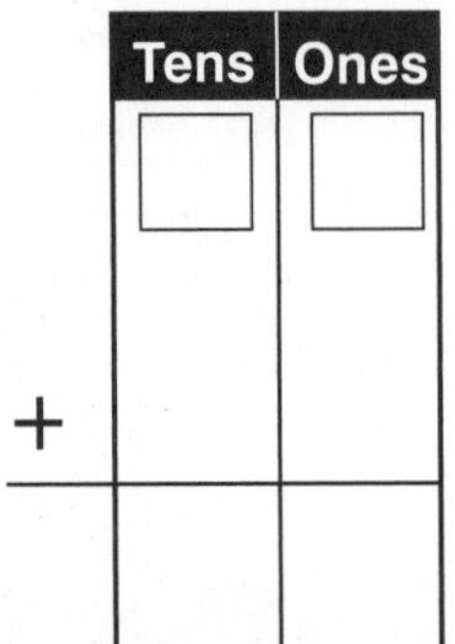

10. 55 + 5

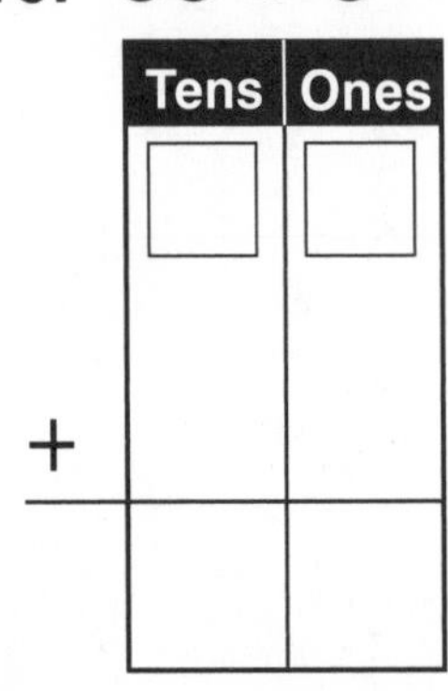

11. 32 + 26

	Tens	Ones
+		

12. 43 + 22

	Tens	Ones
+		

Test Prep

13. Rewrite to add.

36 + 4 =

	Tens	Ones
+		

Use with text pages 289–290.

Name ______________________ Date ____________

Estimate Sums

Round each addend to the nearest ten.
Estimate the sum.

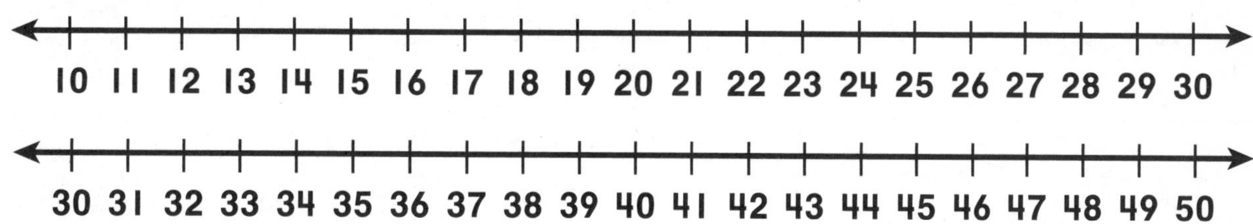

1. 23 + 47

   20 + 50 = 70

2. 12 + 26

   ____ + ____ = ____

3. 25 + 16

   ____ + ____ = ____

4. 38 + 14

   ____ + ____ = ____

5. 17 + 19

   ____ + ____ = ____

6. 49 + 29

   ____ + ____ = ____

7. 45 + 39

   ____ + ____ = ____

8. 25 + 46

   ____ + ____ = ____

Test Prep

Fill in the ○ for the correct answer.

9. Estimate the sum.

   36 + 48

60	70	80	90
○	○	○	○

Name ______________________ Date ______________

Choose a Way to Add

Choose a way to add.
Explain how you find the sum.

1. 42 + 20
   62; Explanations may vary. I used mental math. I just counted 52, 62.

2. 50 + 7

3. 39 + 26

4. 84 + 10

5. 40 + 9

6. 68 + 17 =

Test Prep

7. Fill in the ○ for the correct answer. NH means Not Here.
   Find the sum.

   35 + 30

45	55	65	NH
○	○	○	○

Use with text pages 293–294.

Name ______________________ Date ____________

Add Three Numbers

Remember
Look for a ten or a double.

Add.

1. 15 + 20 + 15 = 50

2. 13 + 50 + 17 = ____

3. 3 + 17 + 21 = ____

4. 13 + 33 + 41 = ____

5. 2 + 38 + 22 = ____

6. 44 + 16 + 5 = ____

7. 63 + 21 + 3 = ____

8. 58 + 21 + 12 = ____

9. 27 + 17 + 10 = ____

10. 8 + 18 + 29 = ____

11. 33 + 22 + 13 = ____

12. 22 + 30 + 8 = ____

Test Prep

13. Will finding a ten or finding a double help you solve this problem? What numbers in the ones column will help you? Write your answers.

56 + 14 + 22

____

____

____

Name ______________________ Date ____________

Practice 11.5

Problem Solving Guess and Check

Use guess and check to solve.

Draw or write to explain.

1. Mrs. Tucker needs 55 buttons for some button dolls that she is making. Which jars should she buy?

   12 and 43

2. The button store sold 58 buttons to the High Street Elementary School. Which two jars of buttons did the school buy?

   ______ and ______

3. Mr. Richards needs 70 buttons for an art project. Which two jars of buttons should Mr. Richards buy?

   ______ and ______

Test Prep

Fill in the ○ for the correct answer. NH means Not Here.

4. Guess and check to solve.

   Zeke bought 50 toy animals for a party. Which two jars of animals did Zeke buy?

22 + 16	22 + 34	34 + 16	NH
○	○	○	○

Name ______________________ Date ____________

Practice 12.1

Mental Math: Subtract Tens

Complete the subtraction sentences.

Remember
Think about subtraction facts.

1. 7 tens − 2 tens = 5 tens

70 − 20 = 50

2. 6 tens − 3 tens = _____ tens

_____ − _____ = _____

3. 9 tens − 5 tens = _____ tens

_____ − _____ = _____

4. 4 tens − 1 ten = _____ tens

_____ − _____ = _____

5. 8 tens − 6 tens = _____ tens

_____ − _____ = _____

6. 9 tens − 2 tens = _____ tens

_____ − _____ = _____

7. 5 tens − 3 tens = _____ tens

_____ − _____ = _____

8. 7 tens − 4 tens = _____ tens

_____ − _____ = _____

9. 6 tens − 2 tens = _____ tens

_____ − _____ = _____

10. 8 tens − 2 tens = _____ tens

_____ − _____ = _____

Test Prep

11. Write the missing number.

9 tens − 6 tens = 3 tens

_____ − 60 = 30

Use with text pages 323–324.

Name ______________________ Date ____________

Practice 12.2

Subtract Tens on a Hundred Chart

Use the hundred chart.
Subtract.

Remember
Move up 1 row for each ten you subtract.

1. 53 − 20 = 33

2. 78 − 30 = ____

3. 62 − 10 = ____

4. 85 − 30 = ____

5. 49 − 30 = ____

6. 74 − 20 = ____

1	2	3	4	5	6	7	8	9	10
11	12	13	14	15	16	17	18	19	20
21	22	23	24	25	26	27	28	29	30
31	32	33	34	35	36	37	38	39	40
41	42	43	44	45	46	47	48	49	50
51	52	53	54	55	56	57	58	59	60
61	62	63	64	65	66	67	68	69	70
71	72	73	74	75	76	77	78	79	80
81	82	83	84	85	86	87	88	89	90
91	92	93	94	95	96	97	98	99	100

7. 57 − 30 = ____

8. 90 − 40 = ____

9. 74 − 10 = ____

10. 61 − 20 = ____

11. 82 − 40 = ____

12. 52 − 10 = ____

13. 68 − 50 = ____

14. 87 − 40 = ____

Test Prep

Fill in the ○ for the correct answer.

15. What number completes the sentence? ____ − 30 = 18

48 ○ 50 ○ 56 ○ 58 ○

Use with text pages 325–326.

Name ______________________ Date ____________

Practice 12.3

Regroup Tens

Use Workmat 3 with [ten rod] and [cube].
Write 1 ten. Write the tens and ones.

Remember
Regroup 1 ten as 10 ones.

1. 73	7 tens 3 ones	Regroup	6 tens 13 ones
2. 57	5 tens 7 ones	Regroup	____ tens ____ ones
3. 65	6 tens 5 ones	Regroup	____ tens ____ ones
4. 86	8 tens 6 ones	Regroup	____ tens ____ ones
5. 49	4 tens 9 ones	Regroup	____ tens ____ ones
6. 54	5 tens 4 ones	Regroup	____ tens ____ ones
7. 92	9 tens 2 ones	Regroup	____ tens ____ ones
8. 70	7 tens 0 ones	Regroup	____ tens ____ ones
9. 34	3 tens 4 ones	Regroup	____ tens ____ ones
10. 81	8 tens 1 one	Regroup	____ tens ____ ones

Test Prep

Fill in the ○ for the correct answer. NH means Not Here.

11. Regroup 4 tens and 1 one.
How many ones are there now?

11	10	5	NH
○	○	○	○

Name ______________________ Date ______________

Practice 12.4

Decide When to Regroup

Use Workmat 3 with [tens block] and [ones cube].

Show the greater number.	Do you need to regroup to subtract?	Subtract the ones. How many tens and ones are left?	What is the difference?
1. 45 − 9	Yes No	3 tens 6 ones	36
2. 68 − 3	Yes No	____ tens ____ ones	
3. 72 − 5	Yes No	____ tens ____ ones	
4. 58 − 8	Yes No	____ tens ____ ones	
5. 92 − 4	Yes No	____ tens ____ ones	
6. 36 − 9	Yes No	____ tens ____ ones	
7. 29 − 7	Yes No	____ tens ____ ones	
8. 81 − 5	Yes No	____ tens ____ ones	

Test Prep

9. Write a subtraction sentence that needs regrouping.

Name ______________________ Date ____________

Practice 12.5

Subtract One-Digit Numbers From Two-Digit Numbers

Use Workmat 3 with [tens] and [ones].

1.

	Tens	Ones
	5	13
	6	3
−		8
	5	5

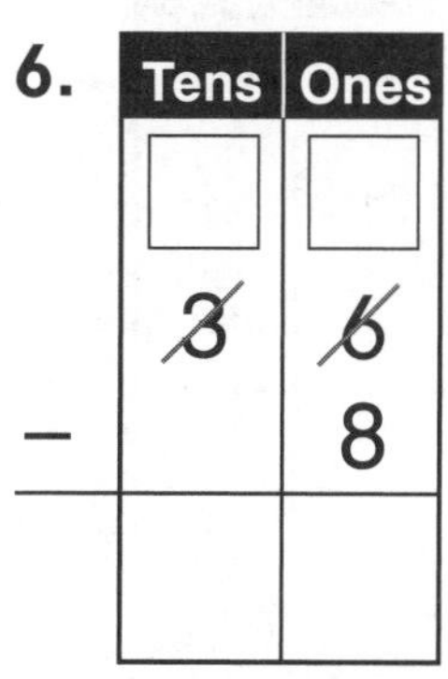

2.

	Tens	Ones
	☐	☐
	4	5
−		6

3.

	Tens	Ones
	☐	☐
	5	7
−		4

4.

	Tens	Ones
	☐	☐
	7	2
−		6

5.

	Tens	Ones
	☐	☐
	8	4
−		9

6.

	Tens	Ones
	☐	☐
	3	6
−		8

7.

	Tens	Ones
	☐	☐
	4	1
−		4

8.

	Tens	Ones
	☐	☐
	5	8
−		7

9.

	Tens	Ones
	☐	☐
	9	3
−		5

10.

	Tens	Ones
	☐	☐
	6	7
−		8

11.

	Tens	Ones
	☐	☐
	7	0
−		6

Test Prep

Fill in the ○ for the correct answer. NH means Not Here.

12. When you subtract 73 − 9, how many ones are in the difference?

0	2	4	NH
○	○	○	○

Name ______________________ Date ____________

Practice 12.6

Subtract Two-Digit Numbers

Use Workmat 3 with [ten-rod] and [unit cube].

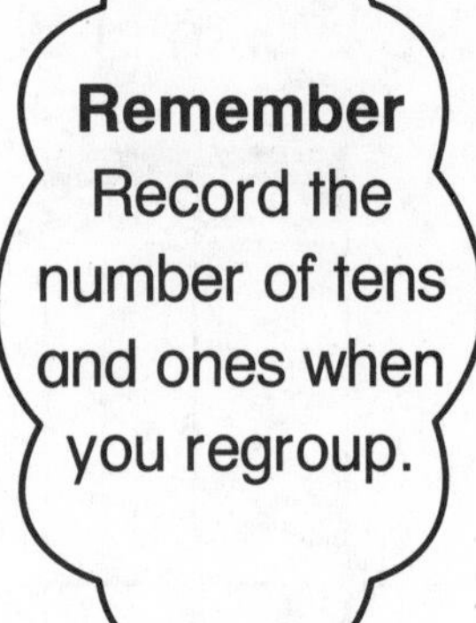

1.

Tens	Ones
4	16
~~5~~	~~6~~
− 2	7
2	9

2.

Tens	Ones
~~3~~	~~4~~
− 1	6

3.

Tens	Ones
7	5
− 3	8

4.

Tens	Ones
~~6~~	~~1~~
− 4	5

5.

Tens	Ones
4	8
− 1	5

6.

Tens	Ones
7	4
− 3	1

7.

Tens	Ones
~~8~~	~~5~~
− 3	8

8.

Tens	Ones
6	3
− ~~1~~	7

9.

Tens	Ones
~~7~~	~~0~~
− 4	5

10.

Tens	Ones
~~9~~	~~5~~
− 2	9

11.

Tens	Ones
6	3
− 4	3

Test Prep

Fill in the ○ for the correct answer. NH means Not Here.

12. When this number is subtracted from 85, it gives you a difference with a 0 in the ones place. What is the number?

15 ○ 20 ○ 30 ○ NH ○

Name ______________________ Date __________

Practice 12.7

Problem Solving
Use a Table

Use the table to solve the problems.

School Fair Food Sales

Foods	Number Sold
Hot Dogs	35
Veggie Burgers	67
Rice and Beans	19
Salads	48

1. The food booth sells food at the school fair. How many more hot dogs were sold than plates of rice and beans?

   Think
   Do I add or subtract?

   16 more hot dogs

Draw or write to explain.

2. How many rice and beans and salads were sold in all?

   _____ in all

3. How many more veggie burgers were sold than salads?

   _____ more veggie burgers

Test Prep

Fill in the ○ for the correct answer.

4. At the fair, 16 children buy juice. 45 children buy milk. How many more children buy milk than buy juice?

   61 ○ 51 ○ 31 ○ 29 ○

Name ______________________ Date ____________

Rewrite to Subtract

Rewrite the numbers. Subtract.

Remember
Line up the ones and the tens.

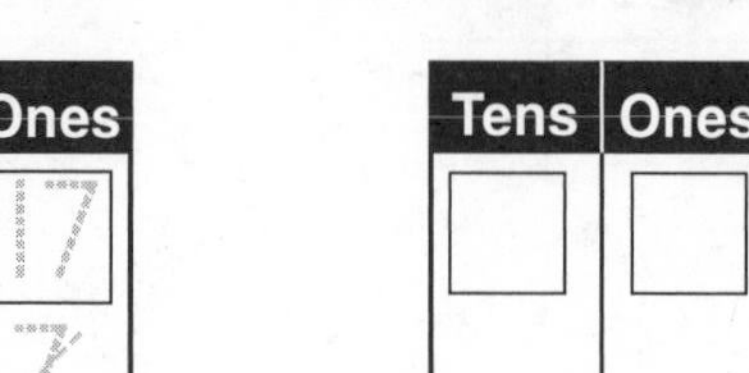

1. 37 − 19

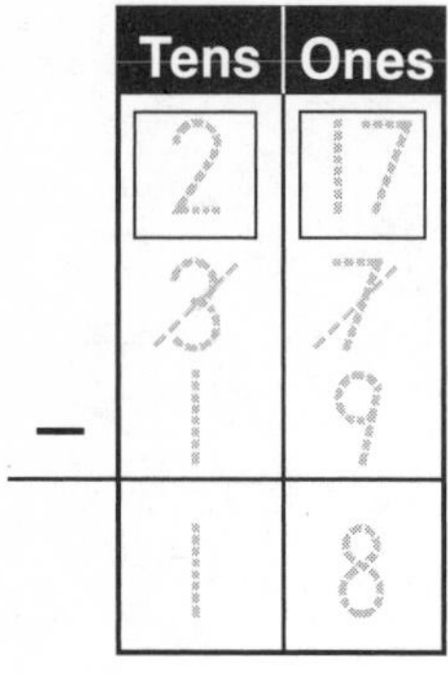

	Tens	Ones
	2	17
	3	7
−	1	9
	1	8

2. 54 − 21

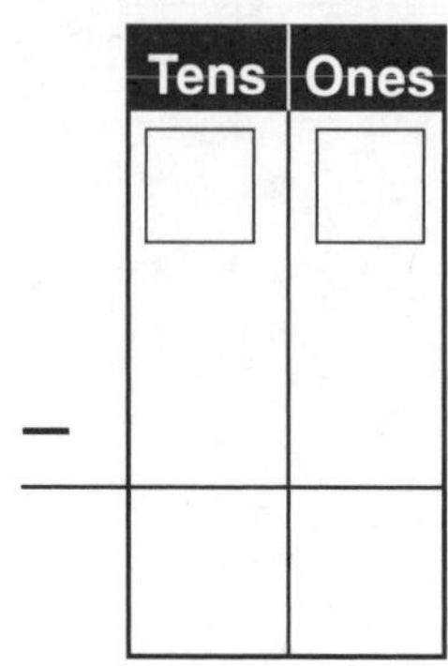

	Tens	Ones
−		

3. 66 − 37

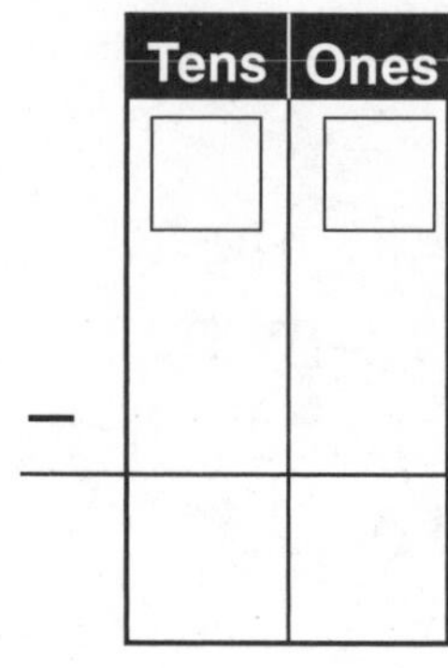

	Tens	Ones
−		

4. 98 − 16

	Tens	Ones
−		

5. 50 − 25

	Tens	Ones
−		

6. 86 − 59

	Tens	Ones
−		

7. 75 − 20

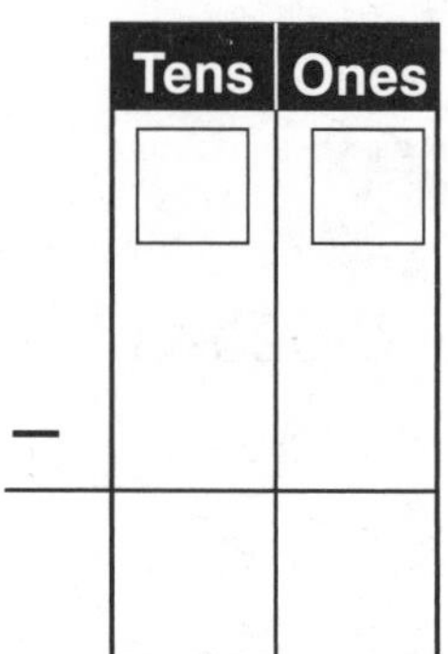

	Tens	Ones
−		

8. 41 − 3

	Tens	Ones
−		

Test Prep

Fill in the ○ for the correct answer.

9. Rewrite the numbers. Subtract.

75 − 36

	Tens	Ones
−		

41 ○ 40 ○ 39 ○ 35 ○

Name ______________________ Date ____________

Practice 13.2

More Two-Digit Subtraction

Subtract.

1.
Tens	Ones
7	12
8	2
− 3	4
4	8

2.
Tens	Ones
4	4
− 2	1

3.
Tens	Ones
9	3
− 6	8

4.
Tens	Ones
6	5
− 3	5

5.
Tens	Ones
3	6
−	5

6.
Tens	Ones
2	5
− 1	8

7.
Tens	Ones
5	8
− 1	9

8.
Tens	Ones
2	6
−	8

9.
Tens	Ones
7	6
− 1	6

10.
Tens	Ones
3	2
−	8

11.
Tens	Ones
5	6
− 2	7

12.
Tens	Ones
5	5
− 1	1

Rewrite the numbers. Subtract.

13. 80 − 8

Tens	Ones
−	

14. 43 − 15

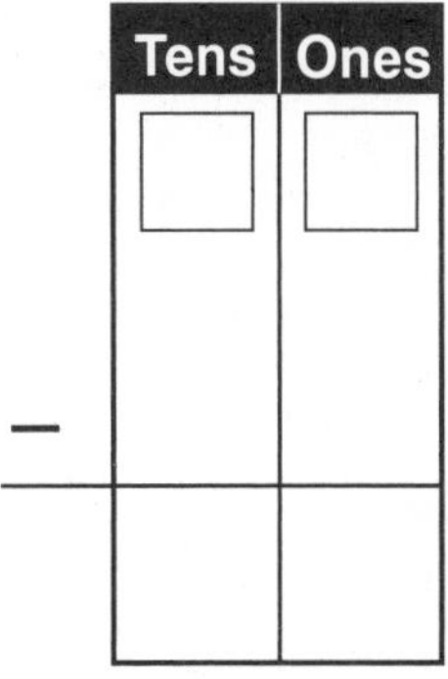

Tens	Ones
−	

15. 61 − 11

Tens	Ones
−	

16. 90 − 5

Tens	Ones
−	

Test Prep

17. Fill in the ○ for the correct answer.

45 − 29

26	17	16	15
○	○	○	○

Use with text pages 349–350.

Name ______________________ Date ______________

Practice 13.3

Estimate Differences

Round each number to the nearest ten.
Estimate the difference.

Remember
Round up if the number has five ones or more.

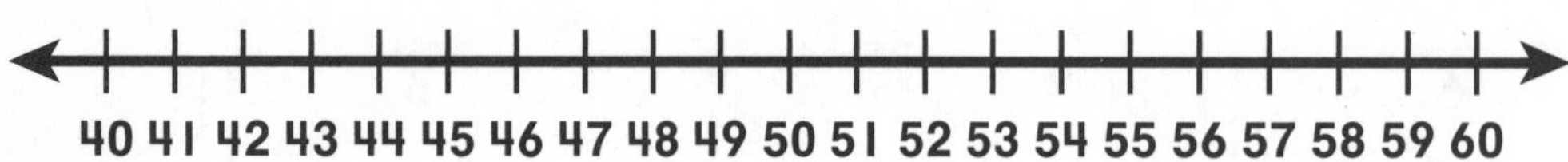

1. 46 − 22

   50 − 20 = 30

2. 55 − 28

   _____ − _____ = _____

3. 44 − 31

   _____ − _____ = _____

4. 56 − 26

   _____ − _____ = _____

5. 45 − 22

   _____ − _____ = _____

6. 38 − 36

   _____ − _____ = _____

7. 43 − 29

   _____ − _____ = _____

8. 49 − 21

   _____ − _____ = _____

Test Prep

Fill in the ○ for the correct answer. NH means Not Here.

9. Estimate the difference.

   56 − 22

30	40	50	NH
○	○	○	○

Name ______________________ Date ____________

Practice 13.4

Choose a Way to Subtract

Choose a way to subtract.

Explain how you find the difference.

mental math
calculator
tens and ones
paper and pencil

1. 56 − 22

34; Possible response: I used paper and pencil so I could line up the tens and ones in the two numbers.

2. 60 − 20

3. 64 − 17

4. 94 − 56

Test Prep

5. Write a subtraction sentence that someone could solve easily with mental math.

____

Name ______________________ Date ____________

Practice 13.5

Use Addition to Check Subtraction

Subtract. Check by adding.

1.
```
  87      19
- 68    + 68
  19      87
```

2.
```
  95
- 10    + ____
```

3.
```
  75
- 58    + ____
```

4.
```
  63
-  5    + ____
```

5.
```
  52
- 10    + ____
```

6.
```
  25
-  6    + ____
```

7.
```
  76
- 12    + ____
```

8.
```
  35
-  5    + ____
```

Test Prep

Fill in the ○ for the correct answer. NH means Not Here.

9. Subtract.

52 – 26

36	26	25	NH
○	○	○	○

Use with text pages 357–358.

Name ______________________ Date ____________

Practice 13.6

Problem Solving
Choose the Operation

Add or subtract to solve.

Draw or write to explain.

1. There are 52 children on two soccer teams. 27 children are on Team A. How many children are on Team B?

   52 (−) 27 = 25

2. The second graders invite 22 third graders and 20 first graders to their class play. How many children do they invite?

   ____ ◯ ____ = ____

3. The art class drew 46 animal postcards and 35 flower postcards. How many postcards did they draw in all?

   ____ ◯ ____ = ____

4. The science class collected 22 sea shells and 10 pieces of sea glass. How many more sea shells than sea glass did they collect?

   ____ ◯ ____ = ____

Test Prep

5. Write to say what math operation you would use.

   The children blew up 25 yellow balloons and 36 green balloons for the party. How many balloons did they blow up? ____________

Use with text pages 359–361.

Name ______________________ Date ____________

Practice 14.1

Pennies, Nickels, and Dimes

Count on to find the value of the coins.

Remember
Count on by
10s, 5s, and 1s.

1.    

10¢ 20¢ 25¢ 30¢ 30¢ total

2.    

___¢ ___¢ ___¢ ___¢ ___¢ total

3.    

___¢ ___¢ ___¢ ___¢ ___¢ total

4.    

___¢ ___¢ ___¢ ___¢ ___¢ total

Test Prep

Fill in the ○ for the correct answer. NH means Not Here.

5. Count on to find the value of the coins.

37¢	27¢	25¢	NH
○	○	○	○

Name ____________________ Date ____________

Practice 14.2

Quarters and Half-Dollars

Count on to find the value of the coins.

1\.  ____¢  ____¢  ____¢ 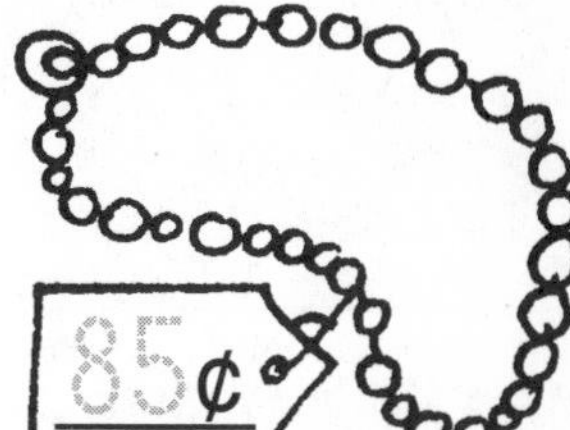

2\.  ____¢  ____¢  ____¢ 

3\.  ____¢  ____¢  ____¢ 

4\.  ____¢  ____¢  ____¢ 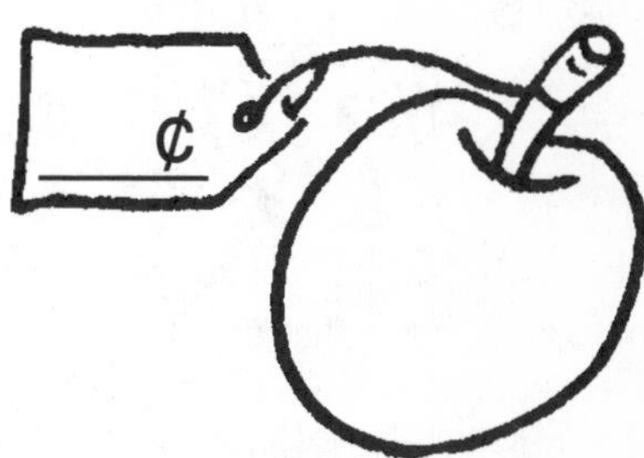

Test Prep

Fill in the ○ for the correct answer.

5\. Count on to find the value of the coins.

80	76	75	26
○	○	○	○

Name ______________________ Date ____________

Practice 14.3

Count Coins

Use coins.

Count on to find the value of the coins.

Remember
Start counting with the coin of the greatest value.

1. 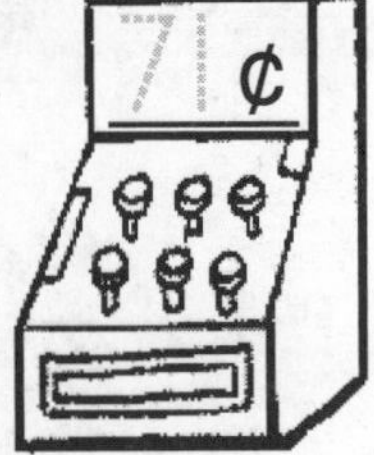 71 ¢   

2. 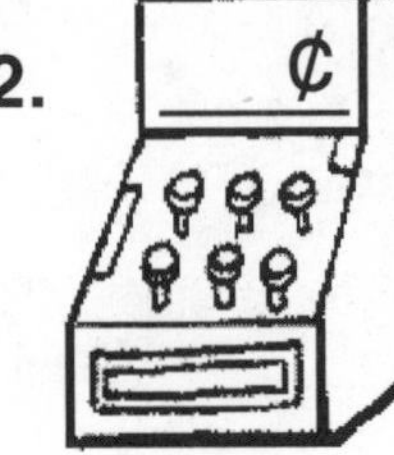 ___ ¢  

3.  ___ ¢   

4. 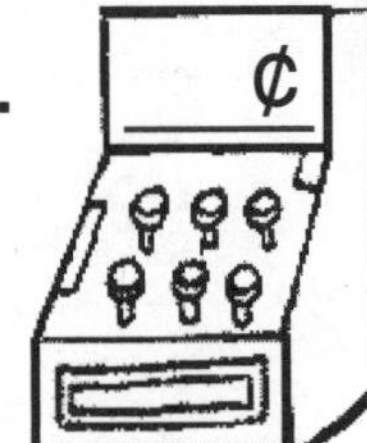 ___ ¢   

5. 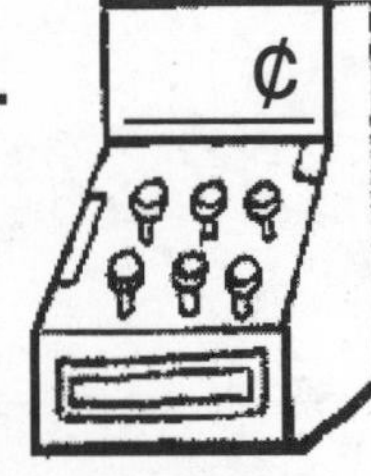 ___ ¢   

6. 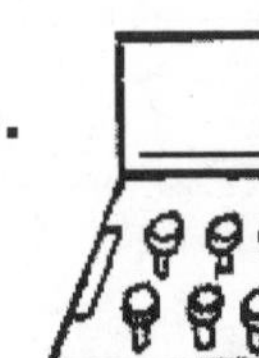 ___ ¢ 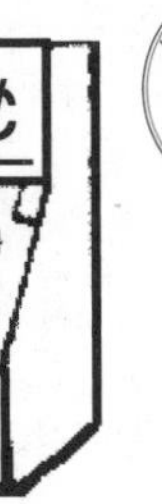   

Test Prep

7. Circle the name.
Who has more money?

Josh

Amy

Name ______________________ Date ____________

Practice 14.4

One Dollar

Write the value of the coins.
Circle the groups of coins that equal one dollar.

Remember Use the dollar sign and a decimal point to write one dollar. Use the cents sign to write amounts less than one dollar, or 100¢.

1. 

$1.00

2. 

____

3. 

____

4. 

____

Find the value of the coins. Circle the correct answer.

5. 

less than $1.00

equal to $1.00

Test Prep

6. Draw dimes to equal one dollar.

Name ____________________ Date ____________

Practice 14.5

Equal Amounts

Use coins.
Show two ways
to make each amount.
Draw the coins.

1. 56¢

2. 56¢

3. 82¢

4. 82¢

5. 95¢

6. 95¢

Test Prep

7. Draw more coins to make the amount 76¢.

Use with text pages 395–396.

Name ____________________ Date ____________

Practice 14.6

Problem Solving Make a List

Make a list to solve.

Draw or write to explain.

1. Chris has only quarters and dimes. How many ways can he make 60¢?

2 ways

25¢	10¢
2	1
	6

2. Jan wants a toy yo-yo for 45¢. She has quarters, dimes, and nickels. How many ways can she make 45¢?

____ ways

25¢	10¢	5¢

3. Mick has only dimes and nickels. How many ways can he make 20¢?

____ ways

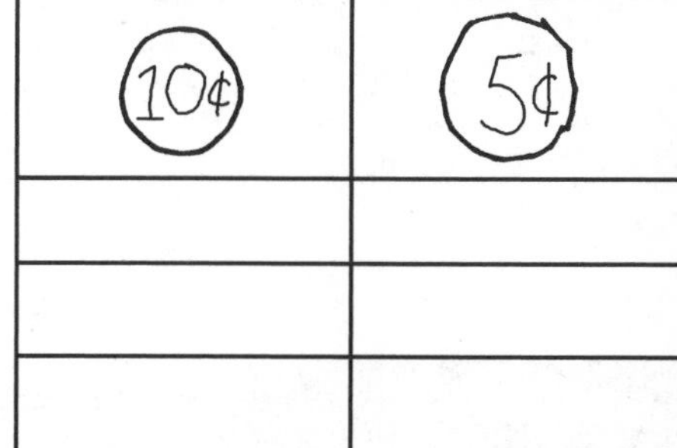

10¢	5¢

Fill in the ○ for the correct answer. NH means Not Here.

4. Rick makes 50¢ with dimes and nickels. If he uses 3 dimes, how many nickels does he use?

6	4	3	NH
○	○	○	○

Name ______________________ Date ____________

Practice 15.1

Make an Exact Amount

Circle the coins that make the exact amount.

1.

2.

3.

Test Prep

Fill in the ○ for the correct answer. NH means Not Here.

4. What amount do these coins show?

48	58	60	NH
○	○	○	○

Name ______________________ Date ____________

Practice 15.2

Compare Money Values

Write the value of the set of coins. Compare.

1. 

40 ¢ (>) 37 ¢

2.  

____¢  ____¢

3.  

____¢  ____¢

4.  

____¢  ____¢

Test Prep

5. Circle the answer.
How does Set 1 compare with Set 2?

Set 1 is ____ Set 2.

less than   greater than   equal to

Set 1

Set 2

Use with text pages 409–410.

Name ______________________ Date ____________

Practice 15.3

Use the Fewest Coins

Remember
Start with the coin of the greatest value.

Find the fewest coins that show the amount. Draw the coins.

1.

2.

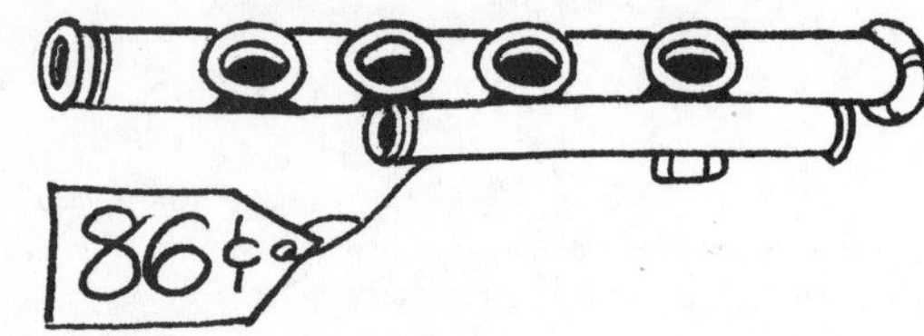

3.

4.

 **Test Prep**

Fill in the ○ for the correct answer.

5. What is the exact amount?
Which coin would you start with for the amount of 98¢?

○ ○ ○ ○

Use with text pages 411–412.

Name ______________________ Date ____________

Practice 15.4

Compare Prices and Amounts

Write the amount of money.
Is there enough? Circle **Yes** or **No**.

1. 24¢		25 ¢ Yes No
2. 92¢		____¢ Yes No
3. 50¢		____¢ Yes No
4. 45¢		____¢ Yes No

Test Prep

Fill in the ○ for the correct answer. NH means Not Here.

5. Which coin do you need to buy the ?

○ ○ ○ ○

Name ______________________ Date ____________

Practice 15.5

Add and Subtract Amounts of Money

Add or subtract.

Remember
Write the ¢ sign in your answer

1.
```
  7 17
  87¢
 −19¢
 ----
  68¢
```

2.
```
  45¢
 +20¢
 ----
```

3.
```
  24¢
 +18¢
 ----
```

4.
```
  99¢
  −9¢
 ----
```

5.
```
  60¢
 +15¢
 ----
```

6.
```
  80¢
 −10¢
 ----
```

7.
```
  59¢
 −15¢
 ----
```

8.
```
  47¢
 +38¢
 ----
```

Rewrite the numbers. Then add or subtract.

9. 62¢ − 17¢ **10.** 49¢ − 26¢ **11.** 33¢ + 17¢ **12.** 27¢ + 9¢

Test Prep

Circle the answer.

13. What is another way to write the numbers?

```
  50¢
 −29
 ----
```

29 − 50 50− 29 29 + 50

Name ______________________ Date ____________

Practice 15.6

Make Change With Pennies and Nickels

Write the amount paid. Draw the coins to find the change.

Amount Paid	Price	Draw Coins to Count On	Change
1.  30¢	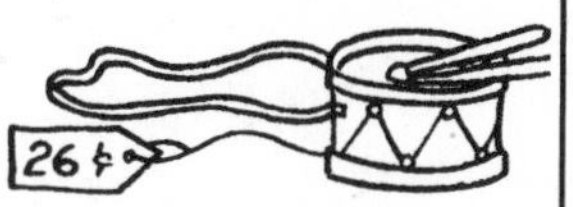 26¢	27¢ 28¢ 29¢ 30¢	4¢
2.  ______	 60¢ ______	______ ______ ______	______
3.  ______	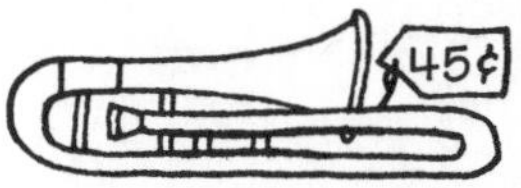 45¢ ______	______	______

Test Prep

Fill in the ○ for the correct answer.

4. Amount Paid: 78¢ Price: 73¢ Change: ?

15¢ ○ 10¢ ○ 5¢ ○ No Change ○

Use with text pages 419–420.

Name ______________________ Date ____________

Practice 15.7

Make Change with Nickels, Dimes, and Quarters

Write the amount paid. Count on from the price to find the change.

Amount Paid	Price	Draw Coins to Count On	Change
1.  75¢	 60¢	70¢ 75¢	15¢
2.  ______	 45¢ ______	______	______
3.  ______	 70¢ ______	______ ______	______
4.  ______	 85¢ ______	______ ______	______

Test Prep

Fill in the ○ for the correct answer. NH means Not Here.

5. Which is the correct change?

Milo pays 65¢.
He buys a little book for 45¢.

20¢	25¢	$1.00	NH
○	○	○	○

Use with text pages 421–422.

Name ______________________ Date ____________

Practice 15.8

Problem Solving
Act It Out With Models

Use coins to act out the problem and solve.

Draw or write to explain.

1. Lucy has 50¢. Then she earns 25¢ watering the plants for her grandmother. How much money does she have now?

   75 ¢

2. Juan has 3 dimes and 1 nickel. How much more money does he need to buy a muffin for 45¢?

   _____¢

3. Bettina has 20¢. How much more money does she need to buy a flower charm for 50¢?

   _____¢

4. Write the answer.
   Draw coins if you wish.

Tommy has 2 quarters and 2 nickels. How much more money does he need to buy a toy for 75¢?

_____¢

Name ______________________ Date ______________

Practice 16.1

Activity: Estimate Time

about 1 hour

It takes about 1 second to touch your toes.
It takes about 1 minute to put on your socks.
It takes about 1 hour to play a board game.

Think about the length of time.
Draw or write things you do that take that long.

1. About 10 seconds
2. About 5 minutes
3. About 1 hour

Test Prep

Circle the answer.

4. How much time would it take to eat lunch?

seconds minutes

Name ______________________ Date ____________

Practice 16.2

Time to the Hour and Half-Hour

Remember
The minute hand points to 12 at the hour. The minute hand points to 6 at the half-hour.

Write the time.

1. 

7:30

2. 

___:___

3. 

___:___

4. 

___:___

Draw the minute hand to show the time.

5. 

5:00

6. 

8:30

7. 

11:00

8. 

2:30

Test Prep

9. Draw a clock.
Then show 4:30.

Use with text pages 435–436.

Name ______________________ Date ____________

Practice 16.3

Time to Five Minutes

Remember
Start at 12. Then skip count by 5s to find the minutes after the hour.

Write the time.

1. 

3:50

2. 

___:___

3. 

___:___

4. 

___:___

5. 

___:___

6. 

___:___

7. 

___:___

8. 

___:___

Draw the minute hand to show the time.

9. 

5:45

10. 

11:00

11. 

2:50

12. 

12:10

Test Prep

13. The times show a pattern. Write the time that comes next.

7:50 7:55 8:00 8:05 ________

Name ______________________ Date ____________

Practice 16.4

Time to 15 Minutes

Write the time.

Remember
A quarter-hour is 15 minutes.

1.	2.	3.	4.
6:15	___:___	___:___	___:___

5.	6.	7.	8.
___:___	___:___	___:___	___:___

Draw the minute hand to show the time.

9.	10.	11.	12.
12:15	3:00	8:45	11:30

Test Prep

Fill in the ○ for the correct answer.

13. What time does the clock show?

7:50	7:55	8:00	6:45
○	○	○	○

Name ______________________ Date ____________

Practice 16.5

Elapsed Time

Complete the times.
Then write how long the sale lasts.

On Sale	Start Time	End Time	How long does the sale last?
FRESH VEGGIES	2:00 P.M.	4:00 P.M.	2 hours
	___:___ A.M.	___:___ A.M.	___ hours
	___:___ P.M.	___:___ P.M.	___ hours

Test Prep

Draw hands on the clock to show that 2 hours have passed.

Name ____________________ Date ____________

Practice 16.6

Use a Calendar

This calendar shows 1 year.
Use the calendar to answer the questions.

1. What is the date one week after May 1? May 8

2. How many months are in one year? ______ months

3. What is the ninth month of the year? ____________

4. What date follows March 31? ____________

5. Which months have 31 days?

____

____

____

____

January 2005

S	M	T	W	T	F	S
			1	2	3	4
5	6	7	8	9	10	11
12	13	14	15	16	17	18
19	20	21	22	23	24	25
26	27	28	29	30	31	

February 2005

S	M	T	W	T	F	S
						1
2	3	4	5	6	7	8
9	10	11	12	13	14	15
16	17	18	19	20	21	22
23	24	25	26	27	28	

March 2005

S	M	T	W	T	F	S
						1
2	3	4	5	6	7	8
9	10	11	12	13	14	15
16	17	18	19	20	21	22
23/30	24/31	25	26	27	28	29

April 2005

S	M	T	W	T	F	S
		1	2	3	4	5
6	7	8	9	10	11	12
13	14	15	16	17	18	19
20	21	22	23	24	25	26
27	28	29	30			

May 2005

S	M	T	W	T	F	S
				1	2	3
4	5	6	7	8	9	10
11	12	13	14	15	16	17
18	19	20	21	22	23	24
25	26	27	28	29	30	31

June 2005

S	M	T	W	T	F	S
1	2	3	4	5	6	7
8	9	10	11	12	13	14
15	16	17	18	19	20	21
22	23	24	25	26	27	28
29	30					

July 2005

S	M	T	W	T	F	S
		1	2	3	4	5
6	7	8	9	10	11	12
13	14	15	16	17	18	19
20	21	22	23	24	25	26
27	28	29	30	31		

August 2005

S	M	T	W	T	F	S
					1	2
3	4	5	6	7	8	9
10	11	12	13	14	15	16
17	18	19	20	21	22	23
24/31	25	26	27	28	29	30

September 2005

S	M	T	W	T	F	S
	1	2	3	4	5	6
7	8	9	10	11	12	13
14	15	16	17	18	19	20
21	22	23	24	25	26	27
28	29	30				

October 2005

S	M	T	W	T	F	S
			1	2	3	4
5	6	7	8	9	10	11
12	13	14	15	16	17	18
19	20	21	22	23	24	25
26	27	28	29	30	31	

November 2005

S	M	T	W	T	F	S
						1
2	3	4	5	6	7	8
9	10	11	12	13	14	15
16	17	18	19	20	21	22
23/30	24	25	26	27	28	29

December 2005

S	M	T	W	T	F	S
	1	2	3	4	5	6
7	8	9	10	11	12	13
14	15	16	17	18	19	20
21	22	23	24	25	26	27
28	29	30	31			

Test Prep

Fill in the ○ for the correct answer.

6. Which month comes first?

September	February	August	July
○	○	○	○

Name ____________________ Date ____________

Practice 16.7

Hours, Days, Weeks, and Months

Use the words in the box.
Write the best estimate for the length of the activity.

Think
About how long each activity usually takes.

hours	days	weeks	months

1. A school day

hours

2. Piano lesson

____

3. Growing taller

____

4. A skiing trip

____

5. Seeds to grow

____

6. A hiking trip

____

Test Prep

7. Write about or draw something that takes weeks to do.

Name ______________________ Date ____________

Practice 16.8

Problem Solving Use a Table

Some second graders help out in the kindergarten room.

Solve. Use the table and a clock to help you.

Second Grade Helpers	
Student	**Time**
Keisha	10:00 to 11:00
Molly	10:30 to 11:30
Jim	1:00 to 1:30
Miguel	1:30 to 2:30

	Draw or write to explain.
1. How long does Molly help in the kindergarten? 1 hour or 60 minutes	
2. The kindergarten teacher asks Jim to help until 2:00. How much more time will Jim help? ____________	
3. When Keisha leaves, how much time passes before Jim comes to the kindergarten room? ____________	

Test Prep

4. Look at the table. Who spends less time on homework?

Claire	Kim
3:00 to 3:30	3:00 to 5:00

____

Name ______________________ Date ______________

Practice 17.1

Nonstandard Units

Find the real object.

Use [paper clip] and [cube].

Estimate the length with each unit.

Then measure.

	Object	Estimate	Measure
1.	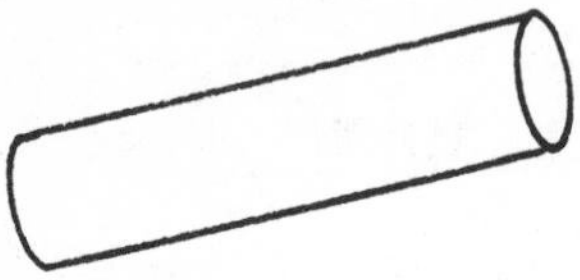	about  ____ [paper clip] about ____ [cube] 	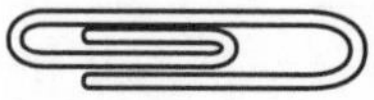 about ____ [paper clip] about ____ [cube] 
2.		 about ____ [paper clip] about ____ [cube] 	 about ____ [paper clip] about ____ [cube] 
3.		 about ____ [paper clip] about ____ [cube] 	 about ____ [paper clip] about ____ [cube] 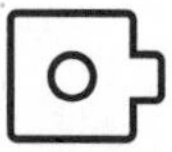
4.	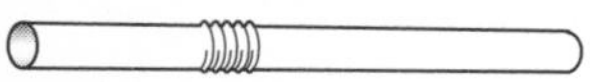	 about ____ [paper clip] about ____ [cube] 	 about ____ [paper clip] about ____ [cube] 

Test Prep

Fill in the ○ for the correct answer. NH means Not Here.

5. About how many paper clips long is this pencil?

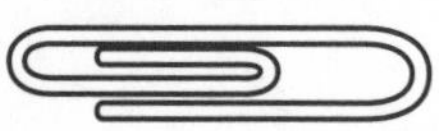

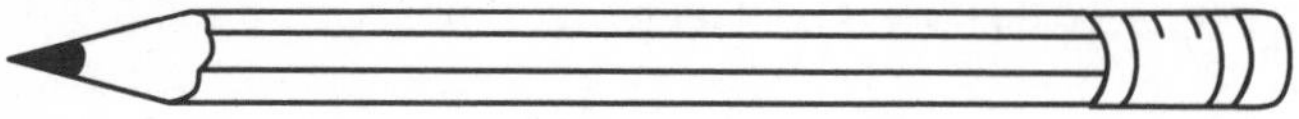

1	3	10	NH
○	○	○	○

Name ______________________ Date ____________

Practice 17.2

Inches

Find the real object. Estimate the length.
Then use a ruler to measure to the nearest inch.

	Object	Estimate	Measure
1.		about ______ inches	about ______ inches
2.		about ______ inches	about ______ inches
3.		about ______ inches	about ______ inches

Write the name of an object.
Estimate its length. Then measure it.

4. ______________ about ______ inches about ______ inches

Compare. Circle the longer object.

5. 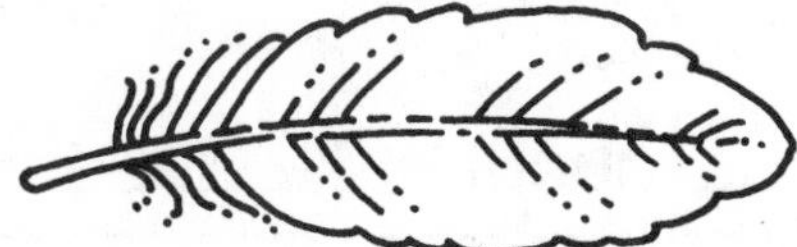 

Test Prep

6. Measure the marker.

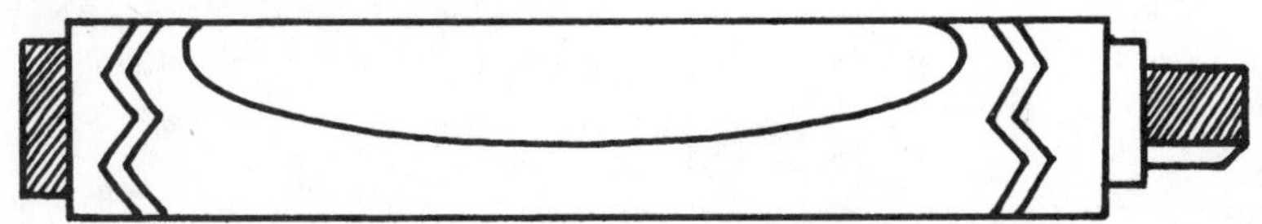

The marker is about _____ inches.

Name ______________________ Date ____________

Practice 17.3

Inches and Feet

Find the real object. Use inches or feet.
Estimate. Then measure.

	Object	Estimate	Measure
1.		about _____ _____	about _____ _____
2.	CALENDAR	about _____ _____	about _____ _____

Draw an object to measure.
Use inches or feet. Estimate. Then measure.

	Draw the object	Estimate	Measure
3.		about _____ _____	about _____ _____
4.		about _____ _____	about _____ _____

Test Prep

Circle the answer.

5. Which is the better estimate for the real object?

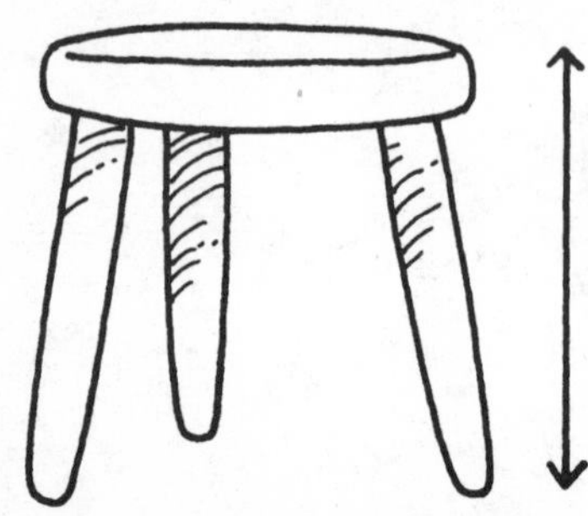

2 inches

2 feet

Name ______________________ Date ____________

Practice 17.4

Foot and Yard

Use feet or yards to estimate the distance.
Then measure.

	Find	Estimate	Measure
1.	How far apart?	about ________	about ________
2.	How wide?	about ________	about ________
3.	How tall?	about ________	about ________
4.	How tall?	about ________	about ________
5.	How wide?	about ________	about ________

Test Prep

Circle the answer.

6. Which is the better estimate for the real object?

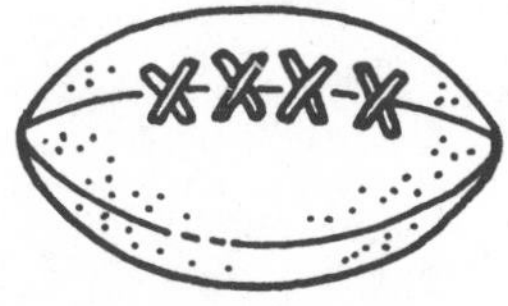

1 foot

1 yard

Name ______________________ Date ____________

Centimeters and Meters

Find the real object.
Use centimeters or meters.
Estimate. Then measure.

Remember
Label your answers with cm or m.

	Object	Estimate	Measure
1.		about ______ ______	about ______ ______
2.		about ______ ______	about ______ ______
3.		about ______ ______	about ______ ______
4.		about ______ ______	about ______ ______

5. Look at the lengths of the four objects you measured. Write the lengths from longest to shortest.

__________ __________ __________ __________

Test Prep

Fill in the ○ for the correct answer.

6. Which is something that would be measured in meters?

shoe	road	worm	hand
○	○	○	○

Name ______________________ Date __________

Practice 17.6

Perimeter

Find the real object. Use a centimeter ruler. Measure and write the length of each side. Add to find the perimeter.

Remember
Measure to the nearest centimeter.

1. 

_____+_____+_____+_____=_____cm

The perimeter is about _____ cm.

2. 

_____+_____+_____+_____=_____cm

The perimeter is about _____ cm.

3. 

_____+_____+_____+_____=_____cm

The perimeter is about _____ cm.

4. 

_____+_____+_____+_____=_____cm

The perimeter is about _____ cm.

Test Prep

Fill in the ○ for the correct answer.

5. Which number is the perimeter?

16 cm	10 cm	6 cm	4 cm
○	○	○	○

5cm

3cm 3cm

5cm

Name ______________________ Date ______________

Practice 17.7

Area

Find the area.
Use square units or grid paper.
Estimate. Then find the area of the shape.

I.

Estimate: about ______ square units

Measure: about ___9___ square units

2.

Estimate: about ______ square units

Measure: about ______ square units

Test Prep

3. Write the word from the box.

inside	around

The perimeter is ______________ the shape.

The area is ______________ the shape.

Name ______________________ Date __________

Practice 17.8

Problem Solving Use a Picture

Use the picture. Solve.

Draw or write to explain.

1. Joan made a paper strip frame for her picture. How much paper did Joan use?

40 cm

2. Barry wants to make a bookmark just like this one. How long will it be? Measure.

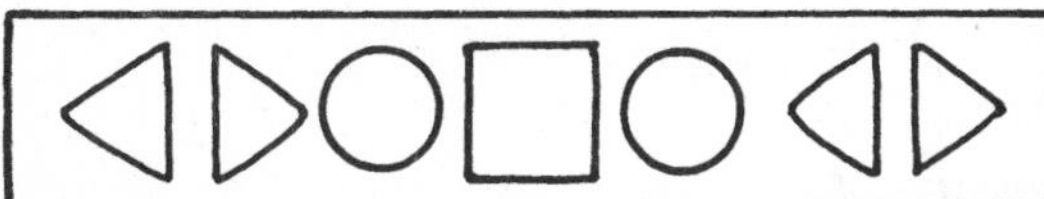

______ cm

3. Lisa wants to put new square patches on her quilt. How many new patches will she need?

______ square patches

Test Prep

Circle the answer.

4. If you want to put down a rug to cover the whole floor in your room, what would you need to find?

perimeter   area

Name ______________________ Date ____________

Practice 18.2

Liters

Find the container.
Estimate how many liters it holds.
Measure.

	Container	Estimate	Measure
1.	bucket	about ____ liters	about ____ liters
2.	vase	about ____ liters	about ____ liters
3.	waste basket	about ____ liters	about ____ liters

Remember
A milliliter is a very small amount.

Circle the better estimate.

4.

10 liters   10 milliliters

5.

50 liters   50 milliliters

Test Prep

Fill in the ○ for the correct answer. NH means Not Here.

6. This cooking pot holds about how much water?

1 liter	10 milliliters	3 liters	NH
○	○	○	○

Use with text pages 511–512.

Name ______________________ Date ____________

Practice 18.3

Pounds

You can measure weight in pounds.

about 1 pound

more than 1 pound

Find objects that weigh more than 1 pound.
Write their names in the table.
Estimate the weight to the nearest pound.
Use a balance and a 1-pound measure to check.

	Object Name	Estimate	Measure
1.	____________	about _____ pounds	about _____ pounds
2.	____________	about _____ pounds	about _____ pounds
3.	____________	about _____ pounds	about _____ pounds
4.	____________	about _____ pounds	about _____ pounds

5. Write the four weights in order from lightest to heaviest.

_____ pounds _____ pounds _____ pounds _____ pounds

Test Prep

6. Circle the answer. Which is the best estimate?

A TV weighs ______________.

about 1 pound less than 1 pound more than 1 pound

Name ______________________ Date ____________

Practice 18.4

Kilograms

Use a balance and 1-kilogram weight.
Complete the table.
Write more than, less than, or about.

	Object	Estimate	Measure
1.	desk	________ 1 kilogram	more than 1 kilogram
2.	sheet of paper	________ 1 kilogram	________ 1 kilogram
3.	dictionary	________ 1 kilogram	________ 1 kilogram

Find objects that weigh more than 1 kilogram.
Write their names in the table.
Estimate. Then measure.

	Object Name	Estimate	Measure
4.	________	about ____ kilograms	about ____ kilograms
5.	________	about ____ kilograms	about ____ kilograms
6.	________	about ____ kilograms	about ____ kilograms

Test Prep

7. Circle the picture.
Which is more than 1 kilogram?

Use with text pages 515–516.

Name ____________________ Date ____________

Practice 18.5

Temperature: Fahrenheit

Write the temperature.

Remember
From one line to the next is 2 degrees.

1.

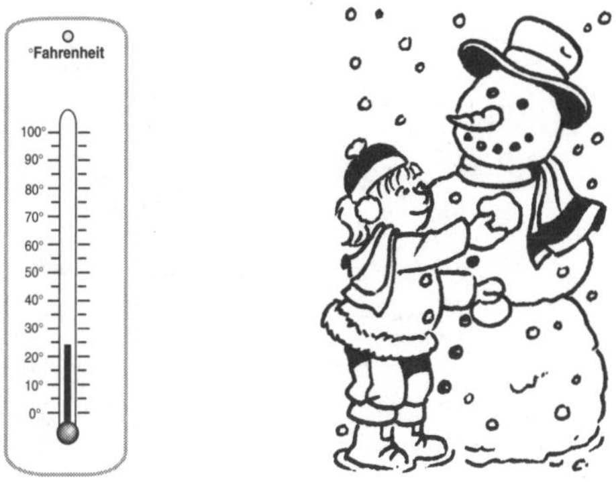

24 °F

2.

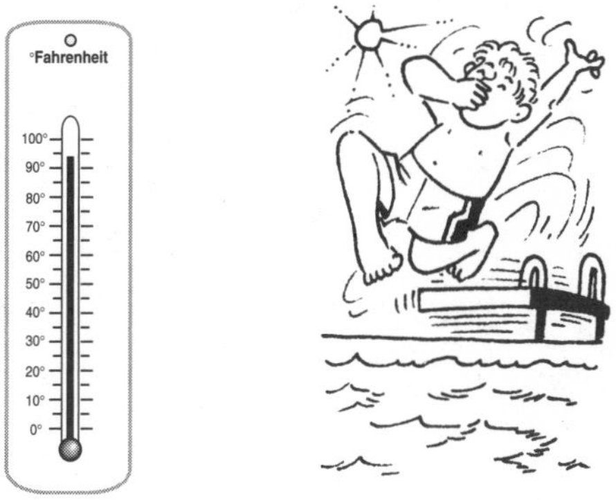

_____ °F

3.

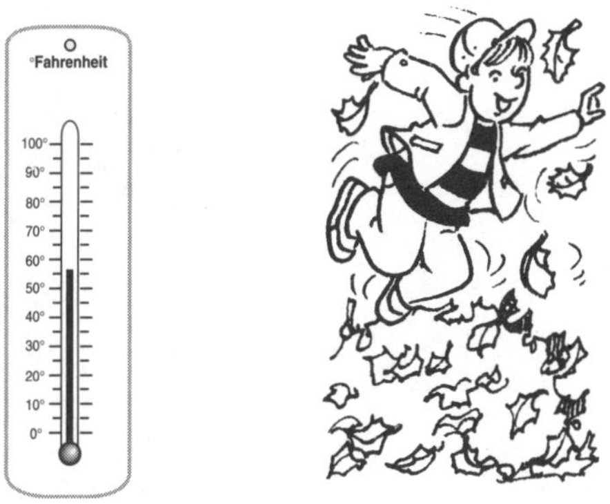

_____ °F

4.

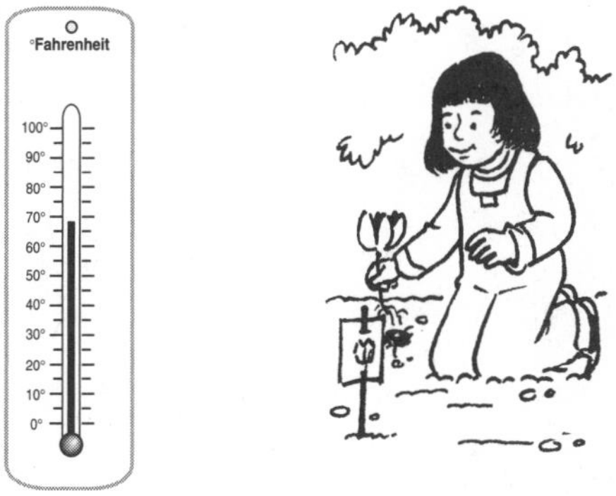

_____ °F

Test Prep

Fill in the ○ for the correct answer. NH means Not Here.

5. What is the temperature?

Rico chooses a coat and mittens to wear to school.

37°F	60°F	75°F	NH
○	○	○	○

Use with text pages 519–520.

Name ______________________ Date ____________

Practice 18.6

Temperature: Celsius

Write the temperature.

Remember
From one line to the next, the temperature changes 5 degrees.

1.

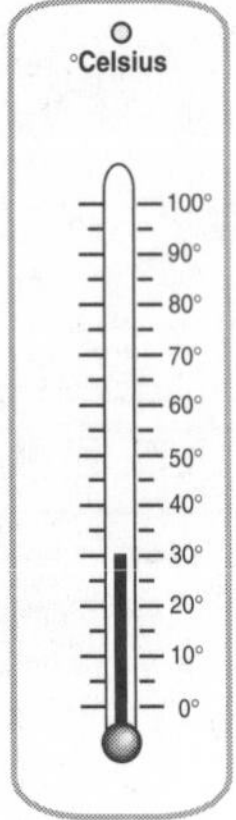

30 °C

2.

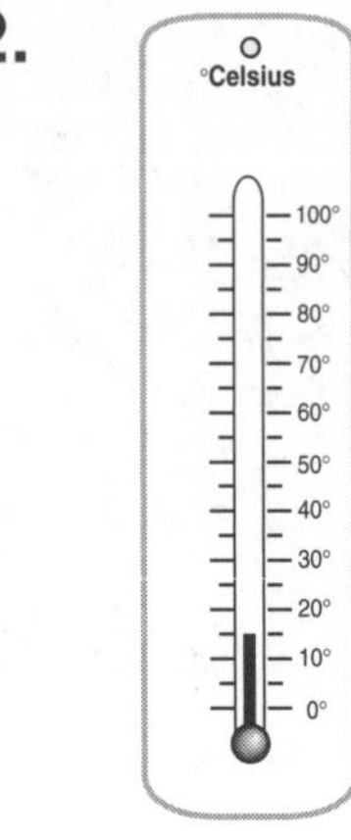

______ °C

3.

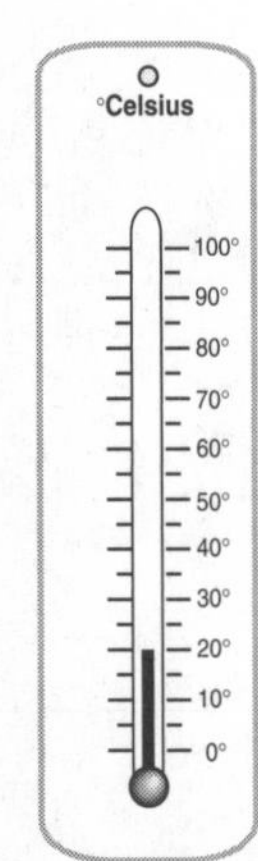

______ °C

4.

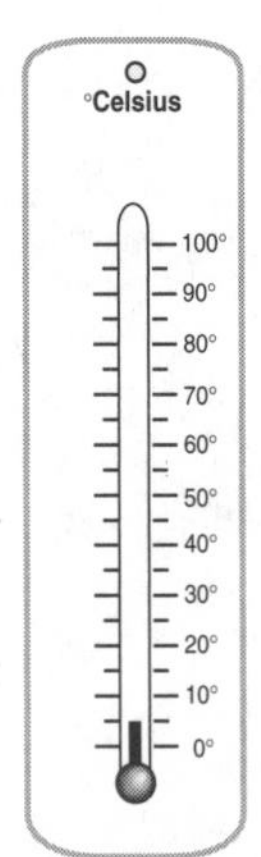

______ °C

Test Prep

Fill in the ○ for the correct answer.

5. Tasha reads a Celsius thermometer. It is a very cold winter day.
Which temperature does she read?

30°C	25°C	10°C	0°C
○	○	○	○

Name ______________________ Date ______________

Practice 18.7

Measuring Units and Tools

Circle the unit needed to measure.
Then circle the correct tool.

Think
What am I going to measure?

1. How heavy is the fruit? 	quart °F inch pound	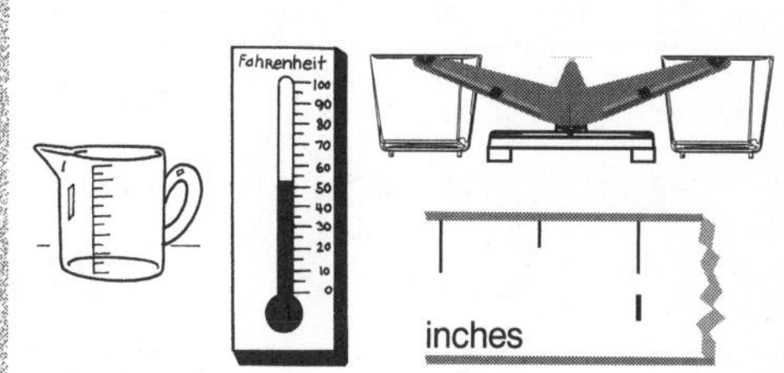
2. How much does the glass hold? 	cup °F inch pound	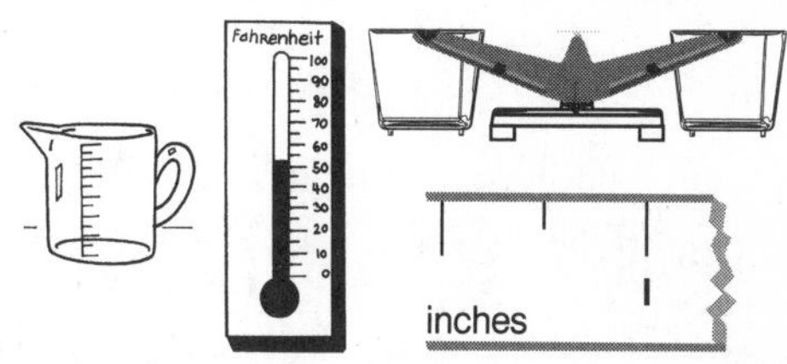
3. How tall is the ladder? 	cup °F inch pound	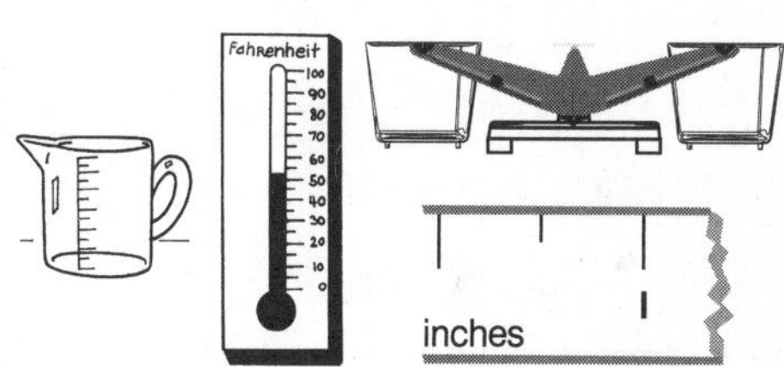
4. What is the temperature today? 	gallon °F inch pound	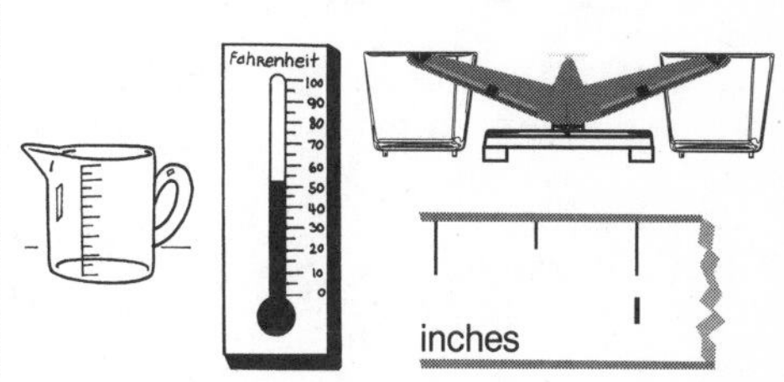

Test Prep

Fill in the ○ for the correct answer.

5. What does the tool measure?

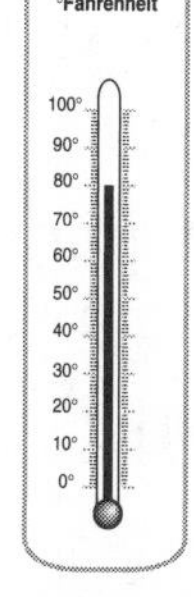

inch	pound	°F	quart
○	○	○	○

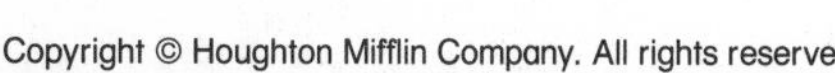

Name ______________________________ Date ______________

Practice 18.8

Decision: Reasonable Answers

Circle the most reasonable answer.

	Draw or write to explain.
1. Sophie makes pink paint for a big mural. She uses a cup of white paint and a few cups of red paint. About how much pink paint does she make? 2 cups 2 pints 2 quarts	
2. Ed measures the paper for the mural. It will be 3 feet tall. It will be about three times as wide as it is tall. About how wide will the mural be? 4 feet 6 feet 9 feet	
3. Steve helps put up the mural in the playground. He puts it up on a sunny day in the fall. What temperature would it be? 30°F 50°F 80°F	

Test Prep

Fill in the ○ for the correct answer. NH means Not Here.

4. Simon pours the juice for the class. He sets out 30 paper cups. About how much juice does he need to fill all the cups?

1 quart	1 gallon	1 pint	NH
○	○	○	○

Use with text pages 525–526.

Name ______________________ Date ____________

Practice 19.1

Exploring Multiplication

Add equal groups, skip count, or multiply to find how many in all.

1. 3 groups of 4

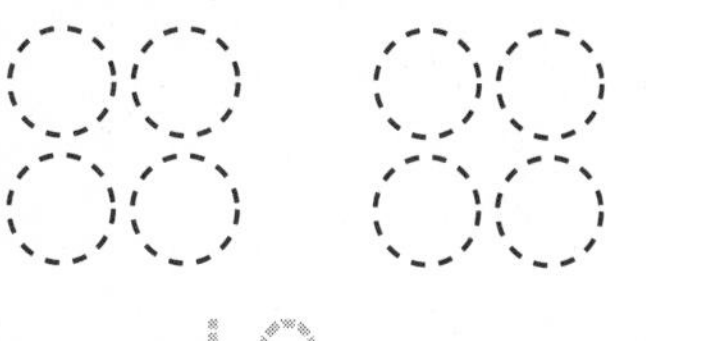

12 in all

2. 2 groups of 5

_____ in all

3. 10 groups of 2

_____ in all

4. 2 groups of 6

_____ in all

5. 2 groups of 4

_____ in all

6. 4 groups of 5

_____ in all

Test Prep

Fill in the ○ for the correct answer. NH means Not Here.

7. Which number sentence does the number line show?

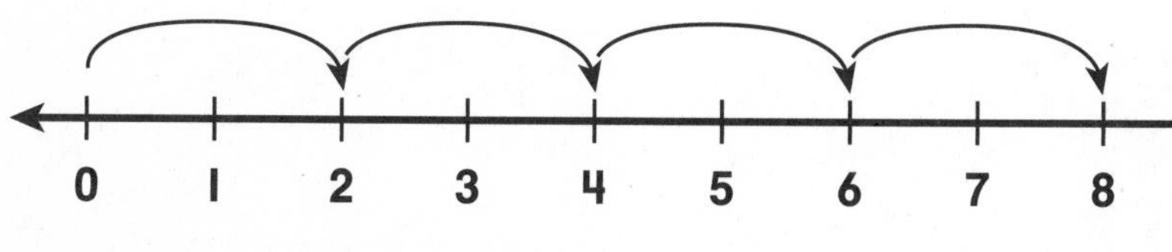

○ 2 + 6 = 8

○ 2 + 2 + 2 + 2 = 8

○ 2 + 4 + 6 + 8 = 20

○ NH

Use with text pages 547–548.

Name ______________________ Date ____________

Practice 19.2

Multiply With 2 and 5

Find the sum. Then find the product.

1. 4 groups of 2

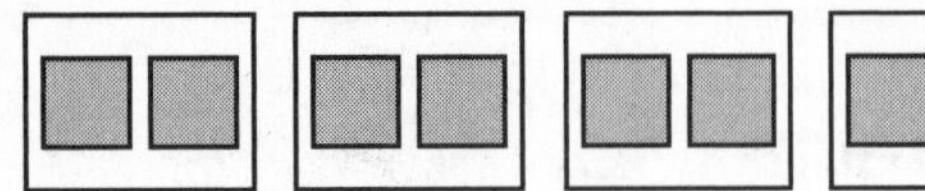

2 + 2 + 2 + 2 = 8

4 × 2 = 8

2. 2 groups of 2

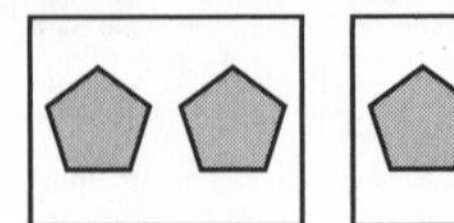

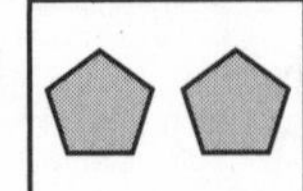

2 + 2 = ______

2 × 2 = ______

3. 3 groups of 5

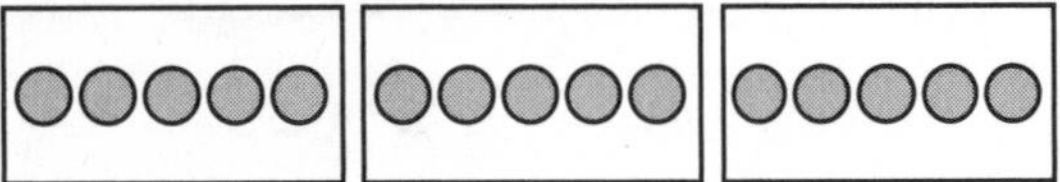

5 + 5 + 5 = ______

3 × 5 = ______

4. 4 groups of 5

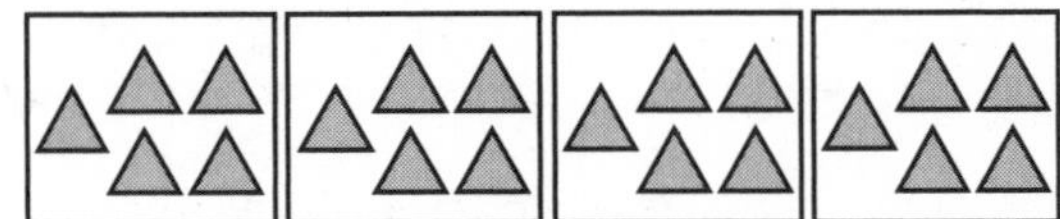

5 + 5 + 5 + 5 = ______

4 × 5 = ______

Multiply.

5. 6 × 5 = ______ 6. 9 × 2 = ______ 7. 9 × 5 = ______

Test Prep

Fill in the ○ for the correct answer.
NH means Not Here.

8. Kayla has 3 boxes of muffins. There are 10 muffins in each box. Which sentence tells how many muffins Kayla has in all?

○ 3 + 10 = 13
○ 3 × 5 = 15
○ 3 × 10 = 30
○ NH

Name ________________________ Date ____________

Practice 19.3

Multiply With 10

Write how many 10s. Multiply.

1. 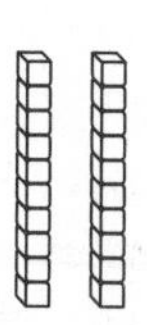

2 tens

$2 \times 10 =$ 20

2. 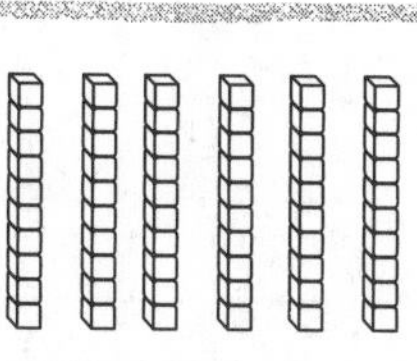

_____ tens

$6 \times 10 =$ _____

3. 

_____ ten

$1 \times 10 =$ _____

4. 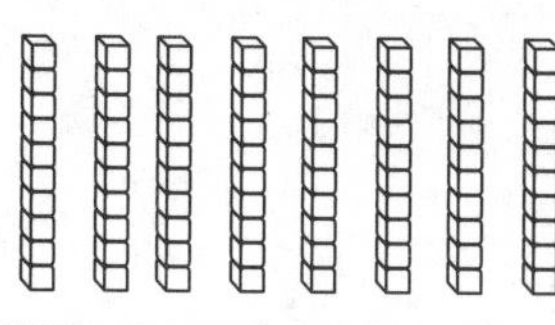

_____ tens

$8 \times 10 =$ _____

5. 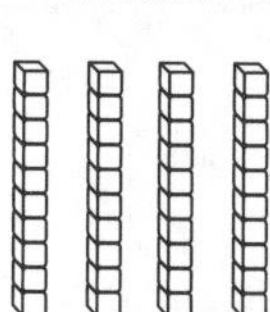

_____ tens

$4 \times 10 =$ _____

Multiply.

6. $3 \times 10 =$ _____
7. $9 \times 10 =$ _____
8. $5 \times 10 =$ _____

Test Prep

Fill in the ○ for the correct answer.

9. Which multiplication sentence tells about this picture?

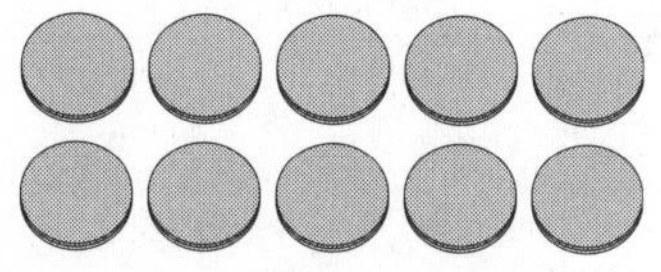

○ $3 \times 10 = 30$
○ $3 \times 5 = 15$
○ $2 \times 10 = 20$
○ $2 \times 4 = 8$

Name ______________________ Date ____________

Practice 19.4

Multiply in Any Order

Color to make equal rows.
Find the product.

1. 3 rows of 2 2 rows of 3

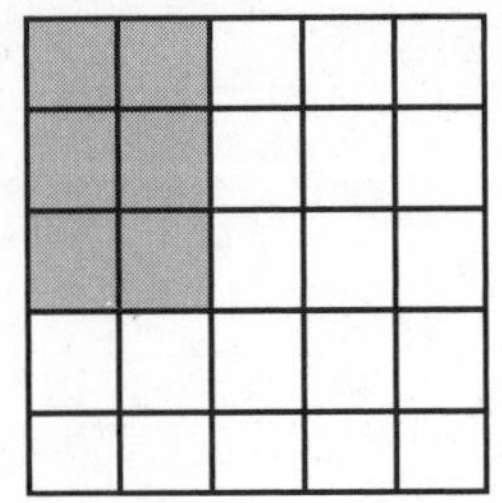

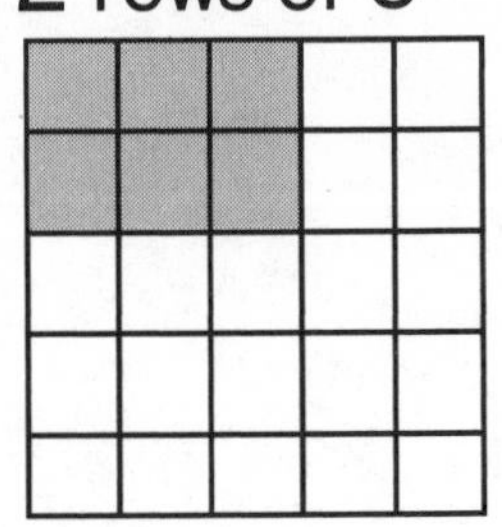

3 × 2 = 6 2 × 3 = 6

2. 3 rows of 5 5 rows of 3

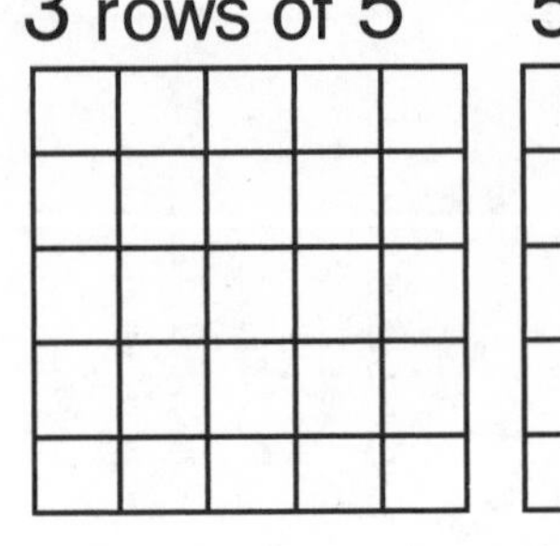

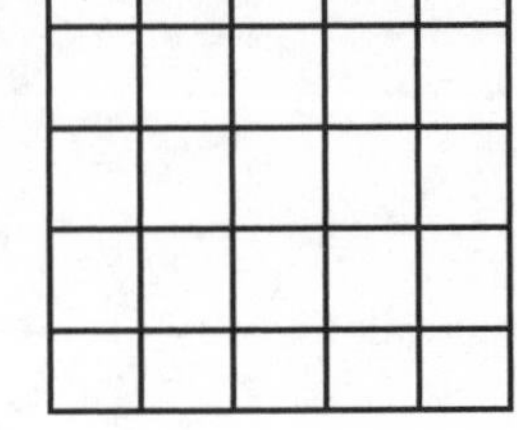

3 × 5 = _____ 5 × 3 = _____

Multiply.

3. 4 × 5 = _____ 5 × 4 = _____

4. 9 × 2 = _____ 2 × 9 = _____

5. 6 × 5 = _____ 5 × 6 = _____

6. 5 × 3 = _____ 3 × 5 = _____

7. _____ = 7 × 2 _____ = 2 × 7

8. _____ = 9 × 5 _____ = 5 × 9

Test Prep

9. Two numbers have a product of 10 and a sum of 7. What are the numbers?

Draw or write to explain.

Name ______________________ Date ____________

Practice 19.5

Share Equally

Use Workmat I and counters.
Draw dots to show the number in each group.
Write how many in each group.

1. 6 counters
3 groups

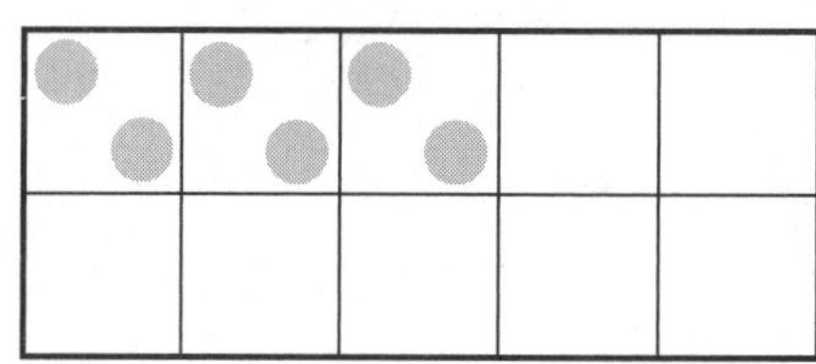

6 ÷ 3 = 2

2 in each group

2. 8 counters
2 groups

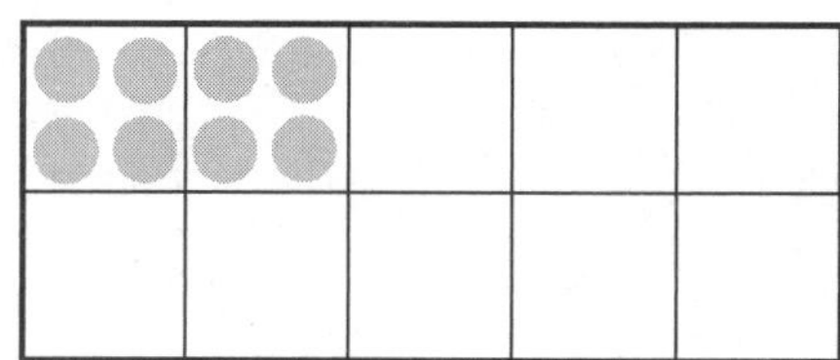

8 ÷ 2 = ____

____ in each group

3. 15 counters
5 groups

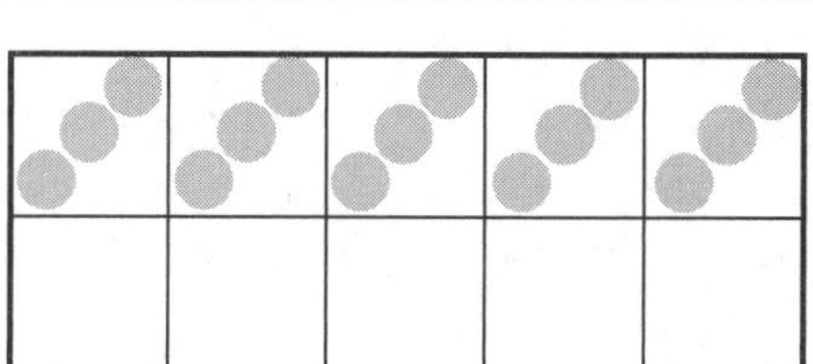

15 ÷ 5 = ____

____ in each group

Test Prep

Fill in the ○ for the correct answer.
NH means Not Here.

4. There are 15 pencils to put in 3 boxes. Bob puts the same number in each box. Which number sentence tells how many pencils are in each box?

○ 15 ÷ 5 = 3
○ 15 ÷ 3 = 5
○ 15 − 3 = 12
○ NH

Name ______________________ Date ____________

Practice 19.6

Equal Groups of 2

Circle groups of 2.
Complete the division sentence.

1. 

16 ÷ 2 = 8

2. 

____ ÷ ____ = ____

3.

____ ÷ ____ = ____

4. 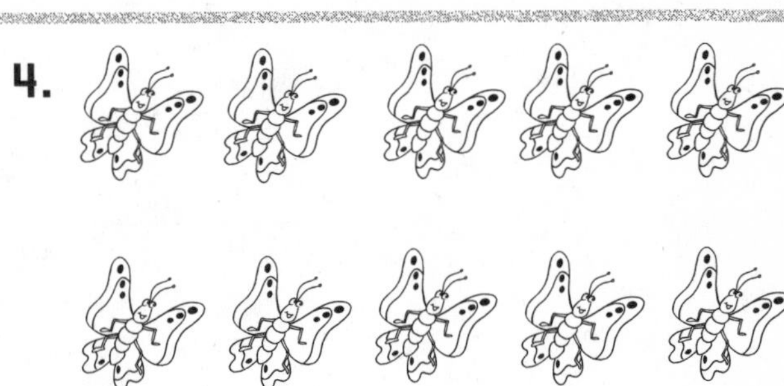

____ ÷ ____ = ____

Test Prep

Fill in the ○ for the correct answer.
NH means Not Here.

5. Use the graph to answer the question. Which number sentence tells how many insects Misha saw?

○ 8 ÷ 2 = 4

○ 4 ÷ 2 = 2

○ 4 × 2 = 8

○ 4 × 1 = 4

Insects In the Garden

Rafi	🐜 🐜
Kayla	🐜 🐜 🐜
Misha	🐜 🐜 🐜 🐜

Key: Each 🐜 stands for 2 insects.

Use with text pages 559–560.

Name ____________________ Date ____________

Practice 19.7

Equal Groups of 5

Circle groups of 5.
Complete the division sentence.

1. 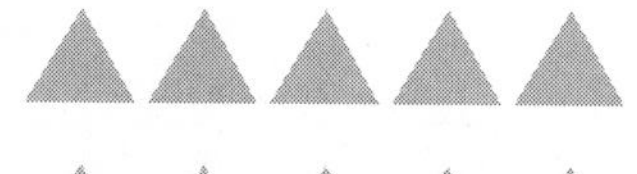
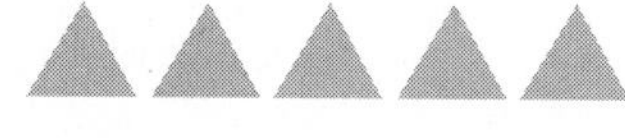

20 ÷ 5 = 4

2. 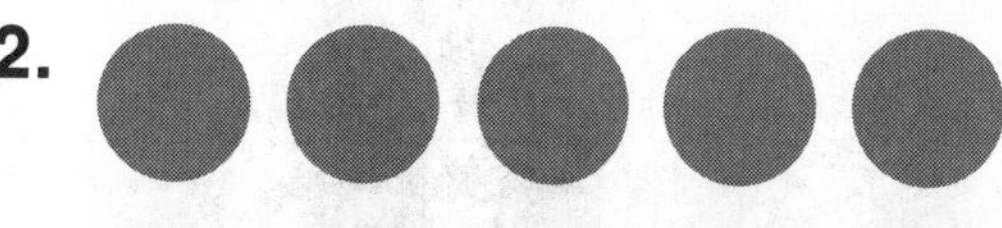
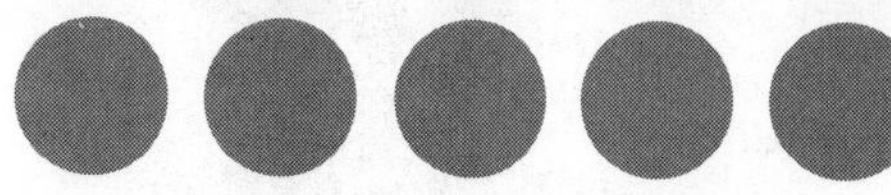

_____ ÷ _____ = _____

3. _____ ÷ _____ = _____

4. 

_____ ÷ _____ = _____

Test Prep

Solve.

5. Annie has 25 flowers to put in baskets. She wants to make equal groups of 5 flowers. How many groups will she make?

_____ groups

Draw or write to explain.

Name ______________________ Date ____________

Practice 19.8

Problem Solving
Draw a Picture

Solve. | Draw or write to explain.

1. There are 5 shirts in Joe's closet. Each shirt has 5 buttons. How many buttons are there in all?

25 buttons

2. There are 6 bags. Each bag has 4 apples. How many apples are there in all?

______ apples

3. Mrs. Super's class has 28 children. The class is divided into 7 equal groups. How many children are in each group?

______ children

Fill in the ○ for the correct answer.

4. Mr. Han makes 20 wooden toys. He puts an equal number of toys in 5 boxes. How many toys does he put in each box?

4 toys	5 toys	15 toys	25 toys
○	○	○	○

Name ______________________ Date ____________

Practice 20.1

Hundreds and Tens

Count by hundreds and tens.
Write the number.

1\.

2 hundreds 2 tens

220 two hundred twenty

2\. 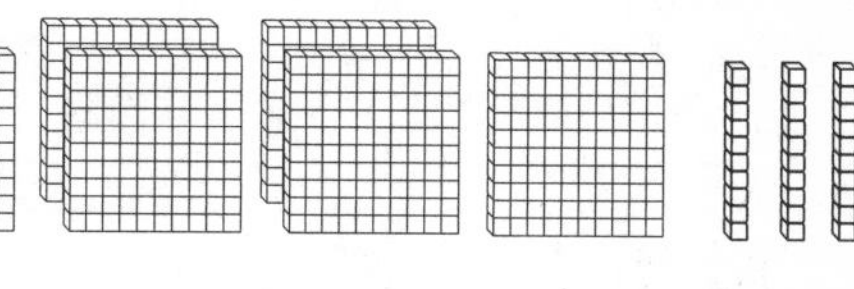

_____ hundreds _____ tens

________ seven hundred thirty

3\. 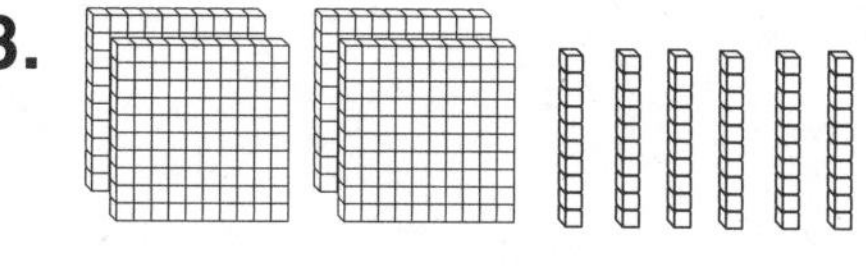

_____ hundreds _____ tens

________ four hundred sixty

4\. 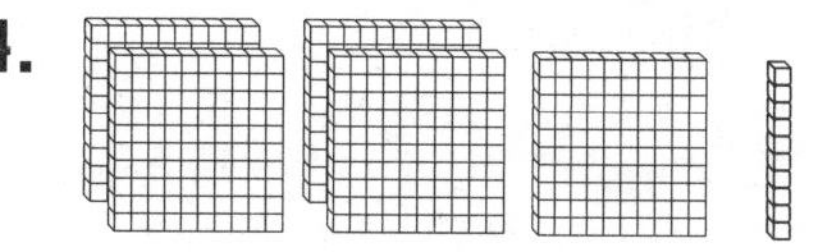

_____ hundreds _____ tens

________ five hundred ten

5\. 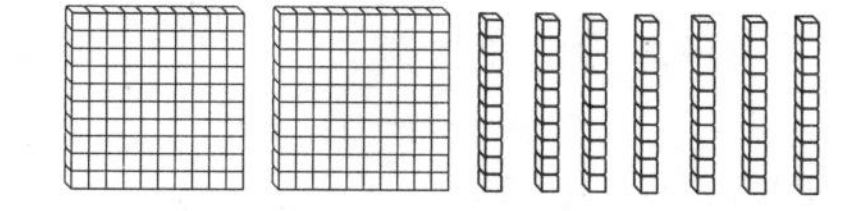

_____ hundreds _____ tens

________ two hundred seventy

6\. 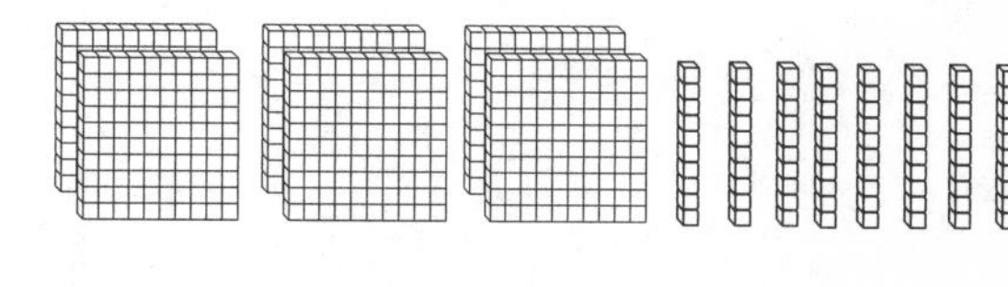

_____ hundreds _____ tens

________ six hundred eighty

Test Prep

Fill in the ○ for the correct answer.
NH means Not Here.

7\. Which number is 100 more than 759?

659	769	859	NH
○	○	○	○

Use with text pages 573–575.

Name ____________________ Date ____________

Practice 20.2

Hundreds, Tens and Ones

Use Workmat 6 with 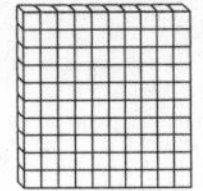, 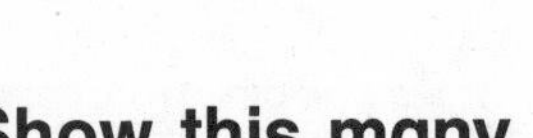, and .

	Show this many.	Write how many.	Write the number.
1.		Hundreds: 1 / Tens: 7 / Ones: 9	179
2.	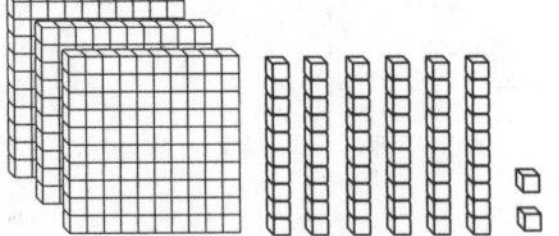	Hundreds: / Tens: / Ones:	______
3.	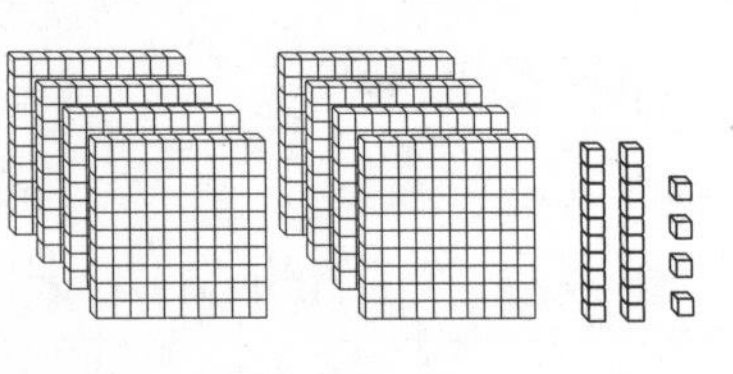	Hundreds: / Tens: / Ones:	______
4.	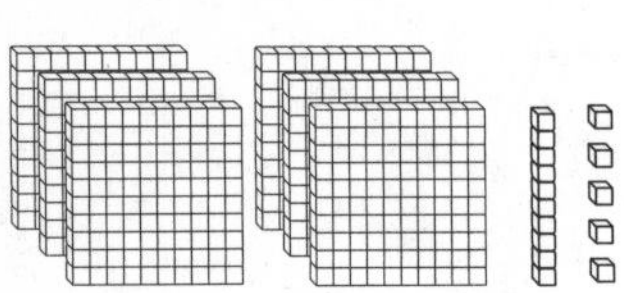	Hundreds: / Tens: / Ones:	______

Test Prep

Fill in the ○ for the correct answer.
NH means Not Here.

5. Which number shows the models?

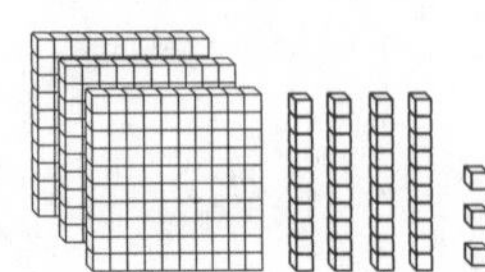

- ○ 300
- ○ 334
- ○ 343
- ○ NH

Name ______________________ Date ____________

Practice 20.3

Identify Place Value to 1,000

Write the number.

1. 7 + 40 + 300 = 347	2. 400 + 8 = ______
3. 9 + 50 + 400 = ______	4. 600 + 20 + 1 = ______
5. 20 + 100 = ______	6. 1 + 30 + 200 = ______
7. 900 + 9 = ______	8. 4 + 50 + 700 = ______

Circle the value of the underlined digit.

To find the value of a digit, find the value of its place.

9. 6̲31	600	60	6	10. 12̲7	200	20	2
11. 503̲	300	30	3	12. 8̲45	800	80	8
13. 29̲0	900	90	9	14. 762̲	200	20	2

Test Prep

Fill in the ○ for the correct answer.
NH means Not Here.

15. What are the missing numbers?

200, 250, 300, 350, ____, 450, ____

○ 350, 450

○ 400, 500

○ 450, 550

○ NH

Use with text pages 579–580.

Name ______________________ Date ____________

Practice 20.4

Read and Write Numbers Through 1,000

Write the number.

1. eighteen 18	2. nine hundred fifty-four _____
3. seven hundred seventy-six _____	4. eighty-two _____
5. nine hundred two _____	6. two hundred forty-two _____
7. thirteen _____	8. eighty-seven _____
9. one hundred sixty-six _____	10. three hundred twenty-nine _____

Circle the word name for the number.

11.	62	sixty-two	ninety-two
12.	684	six hundred eighty-four	eight hundred forty-six
13.	507	fifty-seven	five hundred seven
14.	199	nine hundred ninety-nine	one hundred ninety-nine
15.	567	five hundred sixty-seven	five hundred seventy-six
16.	747	seven hundred forty	seven hundred forty-seven

Fill in the ○ for the correct answer.
NH means Not Here.

17. What is the value of the underlined digit?

2<u>3</u>0

○ two hundred
○ thirty
○ twenty-three
○ NH

Use with text pages 581–582.

Name ______________________ Date __________

Practice 20.5

Different Ways to Show Numbers

Circle another way to show the number.

1. 324	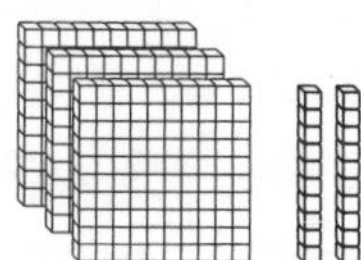	300 + 20 + 4
2. 490	four hundred ninety	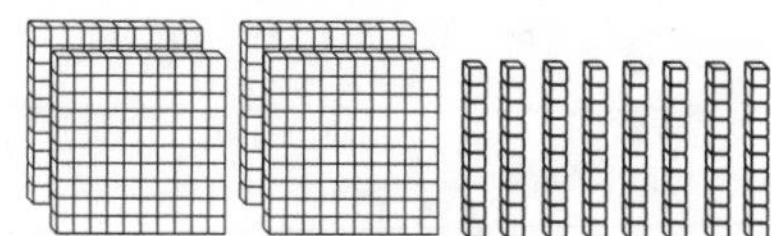
3. 113	100 + 30 + 1	one hundred thirteen
4. 936	900 + 30 + 6	nine hundred sixty-three

Draw or write to show the number another way.

5. 362

6. 203

Solve.

7. Paul has 3 boxes with 100 pencils in each box. He has 4 boxes with 10 pencils in each. He has 1 box with 5 pencils. How many pencils does he have?

Draw or write to explain.

_______ pencils

Use with text pages 583–584.

Name ______________________ Date ____________

Practice 20.6

Before, After, Between

Use the number line.
Write the number.

Before	Between	After
1. 380, 381	393, 394, 395	386, 387
2. ______, 386	391, ______, 393	389, ______
3. ______, 390	389, ______, 391	391, ______
4. ______, 388	385, ______, 387	380, ______

Write the missing numbers.

5. 101, ____, ____, 104, 105, 106, ____, 108, ____, ____

6. 890, ____, ____, ____, 894, 895, ____, ____, 898, 899

7. 23, 24, ____, 26, ____, 28, ____, ____, 31, 32, ____

8. 362, 363, 364, ____, 366, ____, ____, 369, ____, 371

Test Prep

Fill in the ○ for the correct answer.

9. Harry is thinking of 2 numbers. They are between 184 and 187. What are the numbers?

- ○ 183 and 184
- ○ 184 and 185
- ○ 185 and 186
- ○ 186 and 187

Name ______________________________ Date ____________

Compare 3-Digit Numbers

Compare the numbers.
Write >, <, or = in the ◯.

1. 741 (>) 544	2. 913 ◯ 903	3. 460 ◯ 355
4. 799 ◯ 800	5. 429 ◯ 249	6. 850 ◯ 895
7. 510 ◯ 515	8. 100 ◯ 1,000	9. 642 ◯ 642
10. 864 ◯ 846	11. 667 ◯ 695	12. 311 ◯ 113
13. 924 ◯ 924	14. 513 ◯ 351	15. 245 ◯ 204
16. 553 ◯ 535	17. 158 ◯ 851	18. 530 ◯ 539
19. 411 ◯ 410	20. 838 ◯ 850	21. 732 ◯ 711

Test Prep

Solve.

22. Ben's model car traveled 345 feet. Sasha's model car traveled 410 feet. Whose car traveled farther?

_______________ car traveled farther.

Draw or write to explain.

Name ______________________ Date ______________

Practice 20.8

Order 3-Digit Numbers

Write the numbers in order from **least** to **greatest**.

1. 648 700 685 ______ ______ ______

2. 900 967 876 ______ ______ ______

3. 219 109 191 ______ ______ ______

4. 216 203 231 ______ ______ ______

Write the numbers in order from **greatest** to **least**.

5. 267 284 270 ______ ______ ______

6. 714 670 760 ______ ______ ______

7. 983 949 969 ______ ______ ______

8. 610 681 618 ______ ______ ______

Test Prep

Fill in the ○ for the correct answer.
NH means Not Here.

9. Which numbers are ordered from **greatest** to **least**?

○ 510, 516, 524, 532
○ 356, 375, 408, 492
○ 198, 156, 151, 149
○ NH

Name ______________________ Date ____________

Problem Solving Make a Table

Solve.

1. Rachel knits 5 rows on her scarf each night. How many rows does she knit in 5 nights?

Night	1 2
Rows	5 10

Draw or write to explain.

_____ rows

2. Yusef keeps his toy cars in boxes. Each box holds 20 cars. How many cars are in 4 boxes?

Box	1
Cars	20

_____ cars

3. Sharon collects shells at the beach. She collects 11 shells each day. How many shells does she collect in 5 days?

Day	1
Shells	11

_____ shells

Fill in the ○ for the correct answer.

Draw or write to explain.

4. There are 48 muffins to put in boxes. Each box holds 6 muffins. How many boxes of muffins are there?

40 ○ 8 ○ 5 ○ 4 ○

Name ______________________ Date ____________

Practice 21.1

Mental Math: Add Hundreds

Use the basic fact to help you add hundreds.

1. 8 + 1 = 9

8 hundreds + 1 hundred = 9 hundreds

800 + 100 = 900

2. 4 + 4 = ____ | 4 hundreds + 4 hundreds = ____ hundreds | 400 + 400 = ____

3. 7 + 2 = ____ | 7 hundreds + 2 hundreds = ____ hundreds | 700 + 200 = ____

4. 6 + 3 = ____ | 6 hundreds + 3 hundreds = ____ hundreds | 600 + 300 = ____

5. 1 + 4 = ____ | 1 hundred + 4 hundreds = ____ hundreds | 100 + 400 = ____

6. 2 + 6 = ____ | 2 hundreds + 6 hundreds = ____ hundreds | 200 + 600 = ____

7. 4 + 3 = ____ | 4 hundreds + 3 hundreds = ____ hundreds | 400 + 300 = ____

Test Prep

Fill in the ○ for the correct answer.
NH means Not Here.

8. On Monday, 400 people saw the play. On Tuesday, 500 people saw the play. Which addition sentence shows how many people saw the play in all?

○ 4 + 5 = 9 ○ 40 + 50 = 90 ○ 400 + 500 = 900 ○ NH

Name ______________________ Date ____________

Practice 21.2

Regroup Ones

Use Workmat 6 and place value blocks. Add.

1. $\begin{array}{r} \overset{1}{4}03 \\ +\ 58 \\ \hline 461 \end{array}$	2. $\begin{array}{r} 128 \\ +\ 417 \\ \hline \end{array}$	3. $\begin{array}{r} 324 \\ +\ 247 \\ \hline \end{array}$	4. $\begin{array}{r} 543 \\ +\ 126 \\ \hline \end{array}$
5. $\begin{array}{r} 817 \\ +\ 143 \\ \hline \end{array}$	6. $\begin{array}{r} 339 \\ +\ 156 \\ \hline \end{array}$	7. $\begin{array}{r} 145 \\ +\ 7 \\ \hline \end{array}$	8. $\begin{array}{r} 426 \\ +\ 235 \\ \hline \end{array}$
9. $\begin{array}{r} 603 \\ +\ 278 \\ \hline \end{array}$	10. $\begin{array}{r} 754 \\ +\ 28 \\ \hline \end{array}$	11. $\begin{array}{r} 405 \\ +\ 404 \\ \hline \end{array}$	12. $\begin{array}{r} 464 \\ +\ 127 \\ \hline \end{array}$
13. $\begin{array}{r} 453 \\ +\ 119 \\ \hline \end{array}$	14. $\begin{array}{r} 227 \\ +\ 146 \\ \hline \end{array}$	15. $\begin{array}{r} 218 \\ +\ 367 \\ \hline \end{array}$	16. $\begin{array}{r} 785 \\ +\ 208 \\ \hline \end{array}$

Test Prep

Solve.

Draw or write to explain.

17. Mindy has a collection of 342 shells. Ned gives her 39 shells. How many shells does she have in all?

________ shells

Use with text pages 605–606.

Name ______________________ Date ____________

Regroup Tens

Use Workmat 6 and place value blocks. Add.

1. $\begin{array}{r} 187 \\ +\ 131 \\ \hline 318 \end{array}$

2. $\begin{array}{r} 123 \\ +\ 95 \\ \hline \end{array}$

3. $\begin{array}{r} 784 \\ +\ 42 \\ \hline \end{array}$

4. $\begin{array}{r} 261 \\ +\ 346 \\ \hline \end{array}$

5. $\begin{array}{r} 492 \\ +\ 331 \\ \hline \end{array}$

6. $\begin{array}{r} 196 \\ +\ 622 \\ \hline \end{array}$

7. $\begin{array}{r} 387 \\ +\ 130 \\ \hline \end{array}$

8. $\begin{array}{r} 661 \\ +\ 274 \\ \hline \end{array}$

9. $\begin{array}{r} 492 \\ +\ 157 \\ \hline \end{array}$

10. $\begin{array}{r} 381 \\ +\ 457 \\ \hline \end{array}$

11. $\begin{array}{r} 322 \\ +\ 182 \\ \hline \end{array}$

12. $\begin{array}{r} 194 \\ +\ 65 \\ \hline \end{array}$

Rewrite the numbers.
Add.

13. 27 + 792
14. 184 + 161
15. 151 + 92
16. 494 + 465

Test Prep

Solve.

17. A farm truck travels 172 miles to the city. Then the truck drives back to the farm. How many miles does the truck travel in all?

Draw or write to explain.

________ miles

Name ______________________ Date ____________

Add Money

Add.

1. $\$ 4.38 + 1.45$ = $5.83
2. $\$ 1.75 + 3.50$
3. $\$ 6.27 + 0.82$
4. $\$ 1.92 + 7.63$
5. $\$ 8.15 + 1.26$
6. $\$ 4.78 + 2.61$
7. $\$ 4.02 + 2.59$
8. $\$ 5.12 + 3.91$

Rewrite the addends in vertical form.
Add.

9. $5.15 + $1.94
10. $1.90 + $1.99
11. $5.23 + $0.95
12. $5.65 + $3.25
13. $1.86 + $2.05
14. $2.75 + $0.30

Test Prep

Fill in the ○ for the correct answer.

15. Lauren earns money by walking neighbors' dogs. One week, she earned $4.65. The next week, she earned $5.35. How much did Lauren earn for two weeks?

$10.00	$9.00	$5.35	$4.65
○	○	○	○

Name ______________________ Date ______________

Practice 21.5

Problem Solving Guess and Check

Use guess and check to solve.

Remember
If the first guess is not the answer, try two other numbers.

Lunch Menu			
Sandwich	$1.25	Milk	25¢
Slice of Pizza	$1.50	Smoothie	75¢
Salad	$1.00		
Muffin	$1.75		

Draw or write to explain

1. José spent $2.25 for lunch. He got something to eat and something to drink. What did José buy?

slice of pizza and smoothie

2. George spent $2.50 for a drink and food. What two items did he buy?

____

3. Patricia spends $2.50 for four drinks. What does she buy?

____

Test Prep

Fill in the ○ for the correct answer. NH means Not Here.

4. Anne spent $1.90. What did she buy?

muffin and milk	sandwich and smoothie	slice of pizza and milk	NH
○	○	○	○

Name ______________________ Date ______________

Practice 22.1

Mental Math: Subtract Hundreds

Use the basic fact to help you subtract hundreds.

1. 6 − 3 = 3

6 hundreds − 3 hundreds = 3 hundreds

600 − 300 = 300

2.
4	4 hundreds	400
− 1	− 1 hundreds	− 100
	hundreds	

3.
8	8 hundreds	800
− 2	− 2 hundreds	− 200
	hundreds	

4.
7	7 hundreds	700
− 2	− 2 hundreds	− 200
	hundreds	

5.
9	9 hundreds	900
− 8	− 8 hundreds	− 800
	hundred	

6.
5	5 hundreds	500
− 2	− 2 hundreds	− 200
	hundreds	

7.
7	7 hundreds	700
− 3	− 3 hundreds	− 300
	hundreds	

Test Prep

8. The soup factory packs 500 cans on Tuesday and 300 cans on Wednesday. How many more cans does the factory pack on Tuesday?

Draw or write to explain.

_______ cans

Name ______________________ Date ____________

Practice 22.2

Regroup Tens

Use Workmat 6 and place value blocks. Subtract.

1.

H	T	O
	6	10
3	7	0
− 3	3	2
	3	8

2.

H	T	O
7	6	0
− 3	2	8

3.

H	T	O
1	8	3
−	4	5

4.

H	T	O
6	8	1
− 4	1	3

5.

H	T	O
8	5	2
− 4	0	7

6.

H	T	O
3	7	5
− 1	2	9

7.

H	T	O
4	7	5
− 4	1	6

8.

H	T	O
5	2	7
− 1	0	9

9.

H	T	O
4	2	5
− 1	1	6

Test Prep

10. There are 254 third graders at Brown School. There are 229 second graders. How many more third graders than second graders are there?

Draw or write to explain.

______ more third graders

Name ______________________ Date ____________

Practice 22.3

Regroup Hundreds

Use Workmat 6 and place value blocks. Subtract.

1. 645 − 282 = 363 (worked example: 6 crossed out to 5, 4 to 14)

2. 927 − 751

3. 816 − 273

4. 318 − 155

5. 829 − 562

6. 417 − 162

7. 947 − 54

8. 708 − 355

9. 619 − 278

10. 634 − 82

11. 273 − 116

12. 758 − 494

13. 673 − 391

14. 525 − 482

15. 748 − 563

16. 802 − 450

Test Prep

17. Mary has 342 coins in her collection. Lee has 291 coins. How many more coins does Mary have than Lee?

Draw or write to explain.

_______ more coins

Name ______________________ Date ____________

Practice 22.4

Check Subtraction

Subtract.
Check by adding.

1.
```
  8 16
  3 9 6
- 1 5 8
  2 3 8
```
```
  238
+ 158
  396
```

2.
```
  568
- 276
```
+

3.
```
  516
- 475
```
+

4.
```
  826
- 492
```
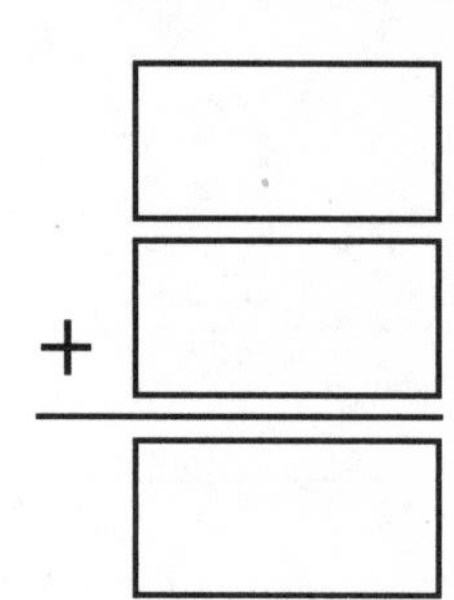

5.
```
  428
- 283
```
+

6.
```
  852
- 503
```
+

Test Prep

Fill in the ○ for the correct answer.

7. Use these digits: 1, 2, 3, 4, 5.
Make the greatest possible sum.
Use each digit only once.

542 + 31	534 + 21	543 + 21	534 + 12
○	○	○	○

Name ______________________ Date ____________

Practice 22.5

Subtract Money

Subtract.

1. $3.55 − 1.70 = $1.85 (example: 2 15)
2. $5.72 − .31
3. $6.37 − 5.19
4. $5.45 − 2.70
5. $8.93 − 2.61
6. $9.50 − .45
7. $6.72 − .53
8. $5.72 − 1.97

Write the subtraction in vertical form.
Subtract.

9. $7.02 − $0.86
10. $1.98 − $0.39
11. $3.68 − $2.95
12. $5.23 − $3.75

Test Prep

Solve.

13. A pasta dinner costs $5.98. A salad costs $1.59. How much more does the pasta dinner cost than the salad?

Draw or write to explain.

________ more

Name ______________________ Date ______________

Choose the Operation

Choose the operation. Write + or −. Then solve.

Draw or write to explain

1. Lee's family drives to Dallas. They drove 342 miles on the first day and 261 miles on the second day. How many more miles did they drive on the first day?

342 ◯ 261 = ______ miles

2. Kim hiked 250 miles last year. She hiked 183 miles this year. How many miles did Kim hike in all.

250 ◯ 183 = ______ miles

3. Martin collected 147 shells at the beach. Sara collected 212 shells. How many more shells did Sara collect?

212 ◯ 147 = ______ shells

Test Prep

Fill in the ○ for the correct answer.

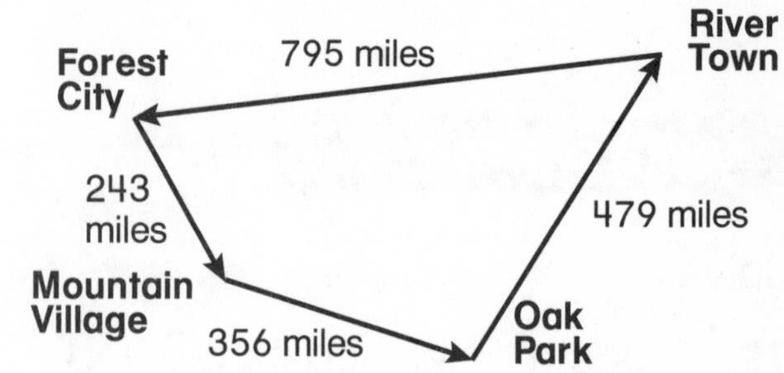

4. Which number sentence tells how many miles it is from Mountain Village to River Town?

○ 479 + 243 = 722 ○ 356 − 243 = 113

○ 479 + 356 = 835 ○ 795 − 479 = 316